C000173125

# *Mindful of Butterflies*

# Mindful of Butterflies

Bernard Jackson and Valerie Baines

Foreword by Roger Tory Peterson

The Book Guild Ltd
Sussex, England

First published 1999


The Book Guild Ltd.
25 High Street,
Lewes, Sussex

Origination, printing and binding in Singapore
under the supervision of MRM Graphics Ltd, Winslow, Bucks

A catalogue record for this book is
available from the British Library

ISBN 1 85776 339 4

# *Table of Contents*

# *Illustrations*

# *Page Decorations*

# *Acknowledgements*

I am indebted to my good friend, Charles H. Cullum, for offering valuable assistance with the original manuscript. To Dr. and Hellen Heller, my appreciation for their encouragement and help. Thanks are also due to Donna O'Driscoll, Olive Butler and Barbara South for typing various stages of the book, particularly the former for her patience and skill in deciphering the original scrawl. Thanks to Dr. David Larson for lending butterfly specimens to help with the artwork and to my colleagues at the Botanical Garden for their determined efforts to keep me informed of butterfly activity around the garden. My wife, as always, offered invaluable support, and read through the final manuscript. I am indebted to Dr. and Mrs. Roger Tory Peterson who showed interest in my efforts and doubly honoured that the late Dr. Peterson, one of the greatest naturalists on earth, provided me with a foreword. A very special thanks to Valerie Baines, the artist and a dear friend, for her meticulous attention to the illustrations and unflagging efforts on our behalf. And last but by no means least, I wish to thank all the people of Newfoundland for giving me the opportunity to work for so many years, with the things I love – flowers and butterflies.

Bernard S. Jackson

# *Foreword*

**by Roger Tory Peterson**

*My first published drawing was a pen and ink of a* butterfly, *not a bird. The* Buffalo Evening News *held a weekly contest for young people, offering a prize of two dollars for the best drawing. I drew a portrait of the White Admiral, then known as the Banded Purple, and titled it "My Favourite Butterfly." The two dollars came in the mail, but my father was not pleased — I had ruined his five-dollar gold-tipped fountain pen.*

*At that time, when I was thirteen, I was deep into butterflies, a passion that over the years has taken second place only to birds. Butterflies, in common with birds, have elegance and beauty; and they fly free.*

*During the past several years my wife, Ginny, has developed a butterfly garden outside my studio. She conceived it when I was suffering an affliction common to artists and writers — creative block. I had been asked to paint a canvas for an important exhibition, but try as I might I could not get a fix on a concept. I agonized for weeks; it had me stymied.*

*Ginny, ever aware of my moods, tried to think of some way to get me over the hurdle. Just looking at the same birds at the feeders outside my studio windows was not the answer. She had noticed that when we were on trips I was as observant and excited about the butterflies as I was about the birds. In an inspired moment she thought, "Why not a* butterfly *garden?"*

*Our home in Connecticut is on 70 wild acres (about 28 hectares), unmanicured except for a rather formal garden at the house. The studio is some 100 yards (90-odd metres) distant on a wooded slope where an abandoned road is used as a thoroughfare for travelling butterflies, which were to be seen only briefly in passage. How to keep them there?*

*Ginny did what any good researcher does — she spent a good deal of time in a library as well as in our own stacks; but she found little that was really helpful on the specifics she needed. There were butterfly gardens in England, she learned; but it was a rather new idea on this side of the Atlantic, although the newly-founded Xerces Society, an organization dedicated to preserving butterflies, was helpful. It was evident that butterflies, like other living creatures, needed primarily two things, food and drink — in their case, food plants for the larvae, nectar for the adults.*

*In the spring of 1979 she started with a small plot at the foot of the studio stairs. Some flowers would be wildflowers, "weeds" if you will, which butterflies need for their larvae. Others would be more showy horticultural blooms irresistible to nectaring butterflies. She wanted, if possible, to have the butterflies living in the garden, or near it, for their entire life cycle. Each year she expanded her efforts, long after I got over my "painter's block."*

*Then, three years into her effort, disaster struck. The man from the heating oil company neglected to watch the hose when the tank in the studio was being filled. During his absence it overflowed and fuel oil spilled over the entire plot. Three years of hard work destroyed!*

*The following spring Ginny dug out all the oil-saturated topsoil and replaced it with fresh earth. Today the butterfly garden flourishes again and is expanding. At least thirty species visit it seasonally, and scarcely a year goes by that some unexpected stray is not spotted.*

*If only this landmark book by Bernard Jackson had been available when Ginny tackled her own project, her task would have been made easier. It is the most informative publication on butterfly gardening we have seen. Its merit is understandable when we consider the qualifications of the author, a distinguished horticulturist who presides over Newfoundland's famous Memorial University Botanical Garden at Oxen Pond. Over the years, while tending his plants, Mr. Jackson simply could not ignore the fragile "flying flowers" not rooted to the earth. He offers us many insights – perceptive ideas based on his daily observations. Because of his full-time involvement he has been able to go into greater depth about butterfly gardening than any lepidopterist.*

*To return to "my favourite butterfly," the White Admiral, I was interested to learn that it has only recently spread eastwards across Newfoundland until it now resides in the St. John's area. Inasmuch as a totally different species in England is known as the White Admiral, I wish we had retained the old name of "Banded Purple," because the insect is really conspecific with the Red Spotted Purple, the bandless form we have in Connecticut. In western New York State, where I grew up, we had both forms. We were in an overlap or "tension zone," and more than once I have seen hybrids or intergrades – individuals with very narrow white bands.*

*Speaking of Admirals, I was astonished to learn that the Red Admiral, which I always thought of as primarily a migrant in the Northeast that originated as far south as Texas and Mexico, actually occurs at times in surprising numbers in the Memorial University Botanical Garden, where it is able to produce plenty of caterpillars because of the presence of its larval food plant, nettles, a recent introduction. Adults are known to hibernate as far north as New York State, but what about those in Newfoundland? Are they able to sustain a viable population, or must they be reinforced yearly from the south?*

*Butterfly watchers anywhere will find a wealth of information in this fascinating book, not only about butterfly gardening and rearing, but also about behaviour, metamorphosis, life history, migration and ecology. Because these chapters are based largely on firsthand observation, they offer insights that will stimulate further research. There is much still to be learned about even our commonest butterflies.*

*A generation or two ago the shotgun or "bird-in-hand" school of ornithology succumbed to the binocular and the telescope. In similar manner, butterfly watching and the camera are now replacing the poison jar, the insect pin and the specimen tray.*

*Read thoughtfully these observations by Bernard Jackson. Enjoy also the visual treat presented by the artist, Valerie Baines, who has rendered three-dimensional compositions of these attractive insects in their own environment, not the usual static, two-dimensional portraits.*

*Watch butterflies more closely; and if you must collect, do it with a close-up lens. Start a butterfly garden, and your local garden club may well pick up the idea. In these days of roadside mowing, spraying and environmental degradation, butterflies need all the help we can give them.*

# Introduction

This book is about butterflies – their natural history, their conservation, and how to attract them to the home garden. By no means should it be considered a definitive work, for much of it simply reflects the results of my own observations, thoughts and experiments.

I have had a love of butterflies since, as a small boy, I watched the clouds of Peacock, Small Tortoise Shell and Red Admiral butterflies jostling for position on the buddleia bushes of home. In those days I lived on the outskirts of Manchester, England. There was a church at the end of our road with its main entrance facing the sun. Somebody, either through luck or foresight, had planted a purple-flowered *Buddleia davidii* against the wall by the big double doors. It was a mecca for butterflies, and since the bus stop was on the adjacent sidewalk, I spent many happy moments, in season, watching the colourful spectacle of literally dozens of butterflies dodging each other and feeding in the warm, sweet-scented air.

That was many years ago. I have since worked as a farmer, a gamekeeper, a Hudson's Bay Company clerk, a government naturalist and wildlife information officer, and goodness knows what else. I have heard timber wolves howling in the night, seen gyrfalcons at their nest, photographed the calypso orchid, smelled the dust kicked up by elephants in the Botswana bush, been overawed by huge douglas firs towering into the sky – but never, never have I lost the pleasure I feel at the sight of a butterfly.

Having inherited a love for gardening from my father, I eventually found myself growing flowers as a hobby and then professionally. For the last twenty-odd years I have been gardening with butterflies in mind. This book is the result.

*When I was a small boy in England, the butterflies were an integral part of the countryside and of our blissful, carefree summer holidays.* Buddleia *bushes graced the private gardens and city park, and sprang up to cover the scars of neglected bomb sites. These shrubs, with their harvest of nectar-laden flower spikes, were irresistible to butterflies, especially to the colourful Nymphalids such as the Red Admirals, the Peacocks, the Painted Ladies, the Small Tortoise Shells and the Comma seen here. These bushes were also a magnet for small boys like me, who had had a love of nature deeply implanted at a very early age.*

Though I watch for butterflies wherever I visit, most of my experience has been in Newfoundland, particularly at the Memorial University Botanical Garden. My having concentrated on one locale may appear on first consideration to limit the practical value of this book for butterfly lovers elsewhere. Not so, for it is the essential thoughts, theories and practices that are important. They are the basis from which to develop one's own local knowledge and personal experiments. We all start from scratch, making errors and enjoying little successes as we go along. I hope this book can eliminate many an early mistake for the beginner and possibly start him or her a few steps ahead of the game.

I believe that one of the best pieces of advice one can give the aspiring butterfly gardener is to locate and study the most reliable sources of local natural history and horticultural information right at the start. Also, it is important to watch butterflies in the wild. See the sort of places they frequent, the type of flowers they visit. Try to find the reasons for what they do, and then use this new knowledge in your garden. Regular visits to the countryside are invaluable. If your garden is in town, however, the information gleaned from watching butterflies in local parks, cemeteries and patches of waste ground may prove even more appropriate.

Read as much as possible on the subject. There are a number of good books available and a steady stream of articles in both the scientific journals and the more popular journals and magazines. Unfortunately, not all writers are practitioners of the hobby, so learn to recognize the names of the reliable ones. It may save you a certain amount of grief!

Do not take everything you read, even from knowledgeable authors, as "gospel." The information they give is probably accurate for their own areas, but it is not necessarily so for yours. For example, I recently read in an article by an extremely knowledgeable and reliable butterfly gardener that the Canadian Tiger Swallowtail lays its eggs so high up in the trees that one rarely sees the eggs or caterpillars. If this author says that such is the case in her area, then it certainly must be so. However, in Newfoundland this butterfly often lays its eggs within 2 metres (6 feet) of the ground, and thank goodness it does, for it gives me the chance to see many eggs and larvae at various stages of their development. There are always exceptions to the rule in nature. Maybe this is one of the reasons why an interest in natural history is so rewarding. It is quite possible for the amateur naturalist to make original and valuable contributions, even if it is simply the recording of every locality where an individual butterfly species is seen or of every type of flower one species visits. All such reporting by reliable observers is valuable and adds to our overall knowledge. Of paramount importance is the fact that every bit of reliable information may one day assist scientists and nature reserve managers in ensuring the continued existence of our butterflies. Should you feel a little sceptical about this comment, let me remind you that, writing to L. Jenyns in 1845, Charles Darwin remarked, "My work on the species question has impressed me very forcibly with the importance of all works as your intended one, containing what people are pleased generally to call trifling facts. These are the facts which make one understand the working or economy of nature."

Bear in mind, though, that scientists and other academics are trained not to accept anything at face value, and become quite fidgety unless presented with irrefutable proof! Indeed, many, sometimes with just cause I am afraid, are inclined to cast a very jaundiced eye at the efforts of the amateur. I grew up with the attitude that such exalted persons, breathing in the rarefied air of academia, were ranked not much lower than the Creator. Over the past number of years, however, I have met many scientists and other experts; indeed, I am fortunate in having some of them as friends. I can assure you that they are not much different from you or me and certainly are not infallible. I have learned that even their findings should on occasion be taken with a large grain of salt. I by no means intend to cast aspersions on their integrity or that of their work. The point, as I said before, is that in the study of natural history (and in other disciplines, for all I know) there is always the exception to the rule, and that no observation, no matter how small, should be discounted out of hand. Twenty-odd years ago an acquaintance of mine was researching a specific aspect of the behaviour of one of the North American ungulates. After seven years of intensive work in the field he was able to formulate a rather interesting hypothesis and so was invited to present a paper at an extremely important conference. Unfortunately, a couple of months before the presentation was due, the animals were observed doing something so totally unexpected that the hypothesis was well and truly shot down in flames! The moral of the story: Do not consider anything you hear about butterflies as the be-all and end-all of it.

Anyway, those of you who may be rank beginners to the art of butterfly gardening, please bear with me as I reiterate the three preliminary steps that I believe should be taken when you are starting on the road to becoming a successful member of this ever-growing fraternity.

First, discover if there is anybody living near you who already has a sound knowledge of the local butterflies. If so, ask that person what butterflies are to be found in the area and which of them are common. If you live in an isolated location, write to your local museum, university, or naturalist club for advice. If you are not already a gardener, then you will have to follow a similar route for information on how to grow the plants you hope to use. In North America, for instance, which has a surface of 20 816 444 square metres (8 037 714 square miles) or thereabouts, possibly the most crucial bit of horticultural knowledge you will need is the rating of your local plant hardiness zone. Once you know this, you can start considering any possible useful plant mentioned in general gardening books, in plant nursery catalogues, or in books such as the one you have in hand.

Second, spend as much time as possible in the appropriate season looking for butterflies in the local countryside or public gardens, parks, cemeteries and other likely places. Try to learn the names of the more common species, not only of the butterflies you see but also of the plants on which they are most often found. Make a note of the date you see them, what they are doing and the type of vegetation they are frequenting. In short, try to learn as much about them as possible. Check a good, detailed butterfly book, and find out in what basic habitat each butterfly belongs. Check for the required host plant of the caterpillars and whether or not the adults migrate. Any practical information may prove of value to you, sooner or later.

Third, only when you have discovered what butterflies are reasonably common in your neighbourhood and the type of habitat they prefer, should you decide which of them you might or would like to attract onto your own piece of land.

These few recommendations hold true no matter in what country or part of the world you live. Certainly it should be clearly understood that the successful attraction or management of butterflies, or of any life form for that matter, depends on sound knowledge of the subject. This is why I stress the first two of my recommendations. But do not be too discouraged if you are starting from scratch; everybody starts with no knowledge at all, and then accumulates some as quickly as possible according to personal interest and effort. Let me hasten to add that you should first attempt to work only with the common, more easy-to-please species, those kinds that many of us refer to as the "backyard butterflies." Any butterfly that is scarce or endangered, or that requires a habitat that is difficult to recreate in the home garden, should be left strictly alone. Its problems can be unravelled only by lengthy and very detailed research. The conservation of such species should be given our moral support but left for the experts to handle.

The beginner's first major problem will likely be learning to identify butterflies. Not to worry, though; most of us will always have trouble trying to sort out the more difficult ones. It is hard enough in a small country such as Great Britain, where there are only about 64 species, but when you think of North America, with somewhere around 695 species, about 250 of which are Skippers, the mind boggles!

After some experience you will no doubt find yourself noticing some semblance of order in the variety of shapes, colours and sizes found in butterflies. You will start to pick out certain groups, the Fritillaries, the Skippers, or the Swallowtails, for instance. From this beginning you will advance to identifying particular species. This is when you will have to consider such things as which of the group have already been found locally and which are usually associated with a particular kind of habitat. Now you will find access to a ready supply of books on butterflies very useful. Even so, because it is a nuisance to haul around any more than just a small book with you on your field trips, you will have to find some reliable way of bringing your observations home with you for checking. Since the memory is never as reliable as we would like to believe, especially for minor details, you need some other method of information retrieval. Though some people now use one of the small modern tape recorders in the field, most amateur naturalists still take a notebook and pencil. There are advantages and disadvantages to both methods, but certainly one great advantage the notebook has over the tape recorder is the opportunity it offers for quick sketches. Even a very crude outline sketch of a butterfly, with arrows emphasizing the various markings and areas of colour, is extremely helpful to your identification of the creature.

Learning to identify butterflies is largely a matter of spending as much time as possible in the countryside, watching them. Of course a good field guide carried along with you helps tremendously. Unfortunately, one of the problems with field guides is that they usually cover far too vast a territory. This can be very tiresome, especially for a beginner. If one is available, a more regional book will eliminate a lot of frustration for you, because such a book deals only with those butterflies likely to be seen in the region and so does away with much of the guesswork.

If you persist in your interest in butterflies, you will probably sooner or later find yourself building up a collection of books on the subject. Though you will, of course, want to study the more advanced books as your confidence grows, I suggest you keep to the basic ones when first starting out on this interesting hobby. Remember that for most of us it is much easier to begin by identifying common butterflies such as the Red Admirals and the Painted Ladies, and by recognizing the various major groups. Groups such as the Blues, the Fritillaries, the Skippers and the Angle Wings can tax even the experts at times. Indeed, I would be very surprised to find more than a handful of people who can accurately identify all the North American Skippers, for instance.

There are some butterflies that are habitually nervous and so rarely allow anybody to approach them closely. I have found a pair of binoculars, the type that can focus on very near objects, invaluable for my observation of these. Some of these butterflies are very small and also close their wings when alighted. Once flushed, they are not always easy to find again, so you will have to develop the skill of mentally marking where an individual went down so that you can relocate it. The Brown Elfin and the Spring Azure are examples of this type where I live. Even some of the larger butterflies are not easily spotted when alighted with their wings closed. I recall once trying to photograph a Grayling butterfly that had alighted on a patch of rocky, sandy soil among some heather in the south of England. Since it would have been fruitless for me to try to approach it standing up, I stalked it by slithering up to the spot on my stomach. This worked fine, but since the Grayling blends into its habitat remarkably well, I very nearly touched it with my nose before relocating it! It is good to remember that a low approach will usually get you a lot closer to any butterfly located within about 1 metre (3 feet) of the ground.

The more confusing butterflies are easier to identify if they are first captured and then carefully examined in the hand. To do this, you need a butterfly net and the ability to capture, remove from the net, and handle these fragile creatures without damaging them. Ways of capturing and handling butterflies and other insects can readily be learned from one of the many books or articles on the topic. Though I am not against the collection of common and non-threatened species for legitimate scientific research, it is not my intention to use this book to further the process. With care, a butterfly captured solely for identification can be released after examination with little or no physical damage. Like birds, butterflies have certain features that are important aids in classifying them. Notice their basic size and shape, and whether the wing edges are smooth, as in the Blues and the Ringlets, or irregular, like the Green Comma and the Compton Tortoise Shell. Do the wings have tails, as do our Swallowtails and the Hairstreaks of Britain? Are the undersides of the wings plain, or do they have spots or other markings? Watching for and recording such features will go a long way towards helping you to identify accurately the species you encounter.

You will by now have realized that butterfly gardening requires more than just the planting of a few colourful flowers. Indeed, I have suggested that the person who consistently has success is the one who takes the trouble to study the butterfly's behaviour and requirements in its natural haunts. Even so, most of us will succeed only with the commoner, less demanding species simply because many butterflies will survive only in their natural habitat. Trying to duplicate the environment of such butterflies in the home garden is fruitless. Even in the wild, discovering their requirements and the reasons for their being where they are will tax the ingenuity of many a present or future scientist.

Anyway, if you are at all like me, you will be only too happy to plod on, making your garden as attractive to these creatures as possible and enjoying any individuals that grace your patch of earth, no matter how brief the encounter may be.

As I said earlier, this book is an attempt to offer the beginner a guide to the fundamentals, theories and practices of butterfly gardening and to the method by which a personal knowledge may be gained. If it can trigger the reader's interest and thoughts and stimulate investigation into the butterflies of his or her own locality, then it has succeeded.

With the world's natural habitats diminishing and so many forms of wildlife becoming endangered at an alarming rate, I believe it is vital for people who are "mindful of butterflies" to begin butterfly gardening now.

*Common Sulphur (*Colias philodice*) on white clover. A few clumps of wild white clover left to flower in some sunny rough corner of your garden will benefit a variety of wildlife, including butterflies and bees.*

*The Compton Tortoise Shell shown here is one of the larger woodland butterflies of North America. The rich colouration of a freshly-emerged specimen defies description. Its subtle tones remind me of those lovely old-fashioned, highly-polished tortoise-shell hair combs one rarely sees nowadays except on the shelves of antique shops. Unless we stop the destruction of our broad-leaved, deciduous forests, this butterfly, along with many others, will quite likely suffer the same fate as the great auk, the passenger pigeon, the blaubok and the Steller's sea cow.*

V.B.

# The Butterfly's Life Cycle

The adult butterfly is the culmination of a four-stage life cycle. Its development is referred to as a complete metamorphosis, and is comprised of the scientifically-named stages of ovum (egg), larva (caterpillar), pupa (chrysalis) and imago (adult butterfly). It may be of incidental interest to note that not all insects pass through a complete metamorphosis. Some, grasshoppers for instance, pass through what is known as an incomplete metamorphosis. These insects have only three major life stages. Their young stages resemble the adult; there is no "resting" stage of chrysalis. Though the average butterfly gardener is at first interested only in luring the free-flying adult into the garden, assisting in the conservation of these beautiful creatures requires a broader interest and a deeper commitment. Since a knowledge of each of the life stages is of some importance for the butterfly conservationist, let us look at each stage separately.

**The Egg** Very few amateurs realize just how beautiful and geometrical a butterfly's egg can be. Very few readers will have ready access to a microscope, but even with a fairly good pocket magnifying glass you can notice differences in shape, size, colour and marking. By examining these characteristics a knowledgeable person can tell accurately to what family of butterfly the egg belongs. For instance, the eggs of the family *Pieridae* – the Whites, the Sulphurs, the Orange Tip, the Brimstone, etc. – have a sort of spindle shape and are usually yellow or orange. They show faint longitudinal lines or ridges. The eggs of the family *Papilionidae*, the Swallowtails, are usually yellow, and are large, round and smooth. When struck by the sun they are reminiscent of tiny seed pearls. The *Nymphalidae* – the Red Admiral, the Painted Lady, the Tortoise Shell, etc. – generally have barrel-shaped, longitudinally-ribbed eggs of a green or aquamarine colour. Many of the *Lycaenidae* – the Blues, the Coppers, the Hairstreaks, etc. – have round, rather flat eggs. They have a pitted texture somewhat like that of a golf ball.

Depending on the species, a butterfly may oviposit, or lay its eggs, singly, in small groups, or in large batches two to five layers deep. They are laid either on or close to the type of plant that is required by the caterpillar for food. Some butterflies, the Red Admiral for instance, lay on top of a leaf, but others, such as the Milbert's Tortoise Shell, lay on the underside. Some species, the Spring Azure and the Holly Blue for example, lay their eggs in among the forming flower head of the host plant. Yet others stick them onto the upright blades of grasses, on a twig, or against the bud of a terminal shoot. The Ringlet and the Marbled White butterflies of Britain and Europe randomly scatter their eggs while in flight over grass. This technique is suitable because the emerging caterpillars are grass eaters and can thereby readily find food. At the other extreme, the Silver Washed Fritillary of Britain deposits its eggs in the crevices of tree bark whence the tiny caterpillar has to go forth and hunt up a supply of its food plant, the dog violet.

Irrespective of where or how they are laid, all butterfly eggs have two things in common. All have a thick shell, the chorion, to protect them from drying out, and all have a small, smooth, circular area, the micropyle, on top or at one end. It is through the micropyle that the egg was fertilized, and through it that air and moisture can pass to the developing embryo.

When depositing their eggs, butterflies use only vegetation that is young, fresh and free from dirt or dust. It is well to remember this when trying to encourage them to breed in your garden. Plants that have been soiled from heavy rain hitting the earth, or smeared with dust from nearby traffic, simply will not tempt female butterflies. The former can be a problem where particularly heavy rain squalls are common, but can be guarded against in your butterfly garden by the use of some form of mulch spread around the plants on the soil surface. The knowledge that dust-covered leaves are avoided by egg-laying butterflies has been put to good use by some Newfoundland vegetable gardeners. When they see the imported Small or Cabbage White butterfly on the wing, they quickly dust their cabbages with flour and thus discourage the insects from laying.

When searching for a place to lay their eggs, female butterflies can be seen flying to and fro over areas of natural vegetation diligently checking for suitable host plants. Though they do not necessarily lay on plants situated in full sun, they all seem to prefer to lay on plants situated in warm, sheltered locations. If you see a female butterfly laying, it will pay you to spend some time watching it to learn just exactly what plant species it is laying on. Let me give you an example.

It was only a few years ago that the White Admiral butterfly extended its range across the island of Newfoundland into my district. Very little if anything was known regarding its breeding behaviour or host plant requirements for Newfoundland. We had to assume that, as elsewhere, it usually oviposited on birch, willow, aspen, or balsam poplar. Indeed, knowing that the butterfly was heading our way, I had already planted a few aspen and balsam poplar for it and had also been busy encouraging our birch and willow. On July 18 of the second summer of the White Admiral's appearance in the Botanical Garden, our assistant horticulturist noticed one paying particular attention to a chuckley-pear (serviceberry or shadbush – *Amelanchier bartramiana*) on the edge of the wood at the back of the perennial border on which he was working. After he told me, I soon located four eggs on the bush, within 1.5 metres (5 feet) of the ground, and possibly missed others. All were on individual leaves, three of them at the very apex. I have seen a number of eggs and caterpillars here each year since then, yet I have rarely found them on any other type of vegetation. The point is that if our assistant horticulturist had not been noticing what was going on around him, we might have spent years searching the more orthodox host plants to no avail.

When you are searching for butterfly eggs, it is well to remember that many species of butterfly appear to favour plants growing on recognized types of flight paths, such as along a woodland edge or lake shore. Many a time have I noticed how a Canadian Tiger Swallowtail will deposit its eggs on host plants it encounters while following a woodland boundary, rather than quarter adjacent open space to lay on isolated, though apparently equally suitable, vegetation away from the woodland edge. The Mourning Cloak or Camberwell Beauty and the Spring Azure in Newfoundland like to lay their eggs on plants jutting out from the shoreline of lakes and ponds, particularly in sunny, sheltered bays. Part of the reason for their choosing vegetation in such sites may be that the host plant sticks out in isolation and is not obscured by other, cluttering vegetation. Certainly there is evidence to show that some butterflies, the Swallowtail of the British Norfolk Broads for instance, require their host plants to project above the surrounding vegetation before they are considered suitable ovipositing sites. This is a good point for the butterfly gardener to bear in mind when placing plants for breeding butterflies. Sometimes the laying of eggs on defined flight paths rather than on other suitable plants close by, may not be in the butterfly's best interests. In a good year, when many butterflies are present and many females are searching for egg-laying sites, this behaviour could result in too dense a population of caterpillars on any one plant. It might incur such disadvantages as an early depletion of food and readier discovery by predators or parasites. Some years ago, in a particularly good Painted Lady season (1979), I had a small clump of viper's bugloss (*Echium vulgare*) growing in a flower bed between the end of a greenhouse and a wire fence. For some reason or other, all the Painted Ladies flying through this "funnel" would stop to lay their eggs on the viper's bugloss, rather than search for the many other suitable specimens located close by. Later in the season I had to hand-pick three dozen well-grown caterpillars from this plant and relocate them, in order to ensure that sufficient browse or green food was left for the twelve or fourteen caterpillars remaining. If I had not done this, they could have starved or have been forced to pupate prematurely. There are, of course, people who believe in letting nature take its course regardless of the consequences, but I feel that, since the garden is already a manipulated environment, we might just as well carry on manipulating things to the advantage of both parties.

The Red Admiral, the Milbert's Tortoise Shell, and possibly other nettle-associated butterflies such as the British Peacock, which follow the edges of nettle beds jutting well out into open fields, can by means of this technique be directed outwards. They can be steered towards isolated nettle patches they would not normally visit. This is, of course, of far more interest to the reserve manager than to the butterfly gardener. These butterflies appear to have a preference for laying close to the very edges of nettle patches, and above all they like to deposit their eggs on plants situated in a depression. In his excellent book *Create a Butterfly Garden*, L. Hugh Newman stated that he was almost certain to find the eggs of butterflies (in Great Britain) where the necessary host plants were growing in a small sand or gravel pit, an overgrown bomb crater, a hollow between artificial banks or hillocks, or simply a natural dip in the land sufficient to provide shelter from the wind. Where winds are frequent, it is particularly desirable for such sites to be available, because butterflies generally avoid windy locations. It is important for the butterfly gardener to bear in mind that one of the main requirements of a butterfly is shelter from excessive wind.

Butterflies inhabiting open flattish countryside such as bogland, prairie, or chalk down, do not have such obvious flight lines to follow, so lay their eggs more randomly throughout the whole area, wherever they find host plants. Shelter from wind is still important, but the sheltered sites are not so apparent. The researcher looking for eggs or caterpillars should investigate suitable plants in slight depressions or on the leeward side of a knoll, rock, or patch of somewhat taller vegetation.

**The Caterpillar** The caterpillars of the different butterflies also vary in colour, shape and size. As with butterfly eggs, by knowing the general characteristics of the caterpillars of each family or group of allied genera, you will have gone a long way towards being able to identify any recently discovered specimen.

Even in a small city garden it is often possible to find a variety of caterpillars. Usually most of these will be the juvenile stage of moths rather than butterflies, because moths far outnumber butterflies both in number of species and in density of population. In Newfoundland the stick and hairy caterpillars seem to be the ones found most frequently. They are usually the larvae of geometrid, tussock, or vapourer moths, not the caterpillars of butterflies. Though there are some tropical species of butterfly of which the caterpillars exhibit coloured tufts of hair, most butterfly caterpillars are not obviously hairy. Some, those of the Blues for instance, have a thin covering of very fine silk hair, and many members of the *Nymphalidae*, including the Red Admirals, the Painted Ladies, the Fritillaries and the Tortoise Shells, are covered in spines, of which some are branched. These hairs, spines, or bristles on caterpillars are referred to as "setae." Apart from the larvae of a few members of the family *Satyridae* such as the Arctics, any densely hairy or tufted caterpillar is likely to be that of a moth.

The time it takes for a caterpillar to develop within the egg varies according to the species of the parent and, to some extent, the prevailing weather conditions. If you happen to see a female lay an egg, you have a very good opportunity to discover just how long it takes for a caterpillar to appear. This is usually only a matter of days. In the Silvery Blue, for instance, it can be as little as 5 days, in the White Admiral 10 days, in the Arctic or Checkered Skipper 9.5 days, and in the Short Tailed Swallowtail 14 days. At the other extreme are butterflies like the Dorcas Copper and the Bog

Copper, or the Purple Hairstreak and the Silver Studded Blue of Britain, that overwinter in the egg stage, a period of about ten months. How such fragile objects can withstand the rigours of winter, especially of a Canadian winter, is beyond me. The egg of the Bog Copper, for instance, is oviposited on *Vaccinium oxycoccus* or *V. macrocarpon*, prostrate bog plants that more often than not are frozen solid under very wet conditions for as long as seven months on end.

Most newly-emerged caterpillars eat all or part of their egg shell immediately on leaving the egg. This supplies a quick shot of energy and so provides them with a favourable start in life. Caterpillars are usually, though not always, found on the leaves, stem, flowers, or forming seed heads of their host or required food plant. There are those, some of the Fritillaries for example, that will leave their food plant when they are not feeding and hide themselves in nearby leaf litter. They are then, of course, much more difficult to locate.

Some caterpillars seem to form an almost uncanny attachment to a particular resting site, to which they return when they are not engaged in feeding. The Tiger Swallowtail and the Short Tailed Swallowtail will return time and time again to a particular site on one of the leaves of their host plant. Over the years I have collected or been given quite a number of these caterpillars, from the wild. They were usually brought in as the result of rescue attempts, and the creatures were placed on similar host plants growing in the Garden, or in pots in my large flight cage. When dealing with caterpillars under these circumstances, it is better not to handle them at all, so I usually cut away most of the leaf on which they are attached, and fix it to a fresh-growing leaf by the simple method of pushing a straight pin through both leaves until they are brought flush with each other. I have noticed that the caterpillars, especially if quite young, will use the small piece of collected leaf as their resting site; they will often move to adjacent leaves to feed, but they always return to the tiny bit of original leaf to rest up. A more usual example of this sort of thing can be seen in the behaviour of the White Admiral caterpillar, which, until it enters into hibernation, always spends its time between feeding lying lengthways along the midrib of the leaf it is eating. It also eats away at the material along both sides of the midrib so that eventually this central vein sticks out from the rest of the leaf like a tank antenna. One would expect caterpillars in such situations to stand out like sore thumbs, but they are surprisingly difficult to locate.

*The White Admiral is one of the most beautiful of woodland butterflies. It is particularly interesting because its caterpillar, unlike those of most other butterflies, overwinters in a leaf tube called a "hibernaculum." This winter shelter is constructed by the tiny caterpillar from a leaf of the host plant, in this case chuckley-pear (*Amelanchier bartramiana*). In the spring, if all has gone well, the caterpillar leaves the hibernaculum and starts on an eating binge. It pupates when fully grown, and it appears as an adult butterfly around mid-July. It will visit the garden if suitable host plants are present and if you are close enough to its natural habitat.*

Though many caterpillars are inclined to lead a fairly sedentary life, some species are remarkably mobile. I have already mentioned that the caterpillars of some species actually vacate the plant while not engaged in feeding. Others transfer from one plant to another as the browse becomes depleted. Such plants need not be rubbing shoulders with each other, either. I have seen a brood of Mourning Cloak caterpillars move off a small willow bush growing in a rough meadow and relocate themselves on another such willow a short distance away. The willows were quite isolated, so how on earth the caterpillars were able to leave one and locate on the other I don't know. Maybe it was just pure luck that they happened to strike out in the right direction. Presumably any such transfer from one plant to another must be done quickly; otherwise, the caterpillar's growth could be retarded, or worse still, the caterpillar could die. The mobility of caterpillars is best demonstrated when they are fully grown and are searching for a place to pupate. At these times it is quite common to see them hurrying along footpaths, across flower beds and so on, in a most purposeful manner. If you happen to capture one to hand-rear, or if you simply put it back on a nearby plant, it will not settle down to feed, but will continue to rush around in a frantic attempt to get to wherever it was heading. If a fully-grown caterpillar in captivity starts behaving in this manner, you can be sure it is needing a suitable place to pupate.

Though the caterpillars of many species, the Pink Edged Sulphur, the Green Comma and the Red Admiral, for instance, are solitary, other species are gregarious. The Pearl Crescent of North America and the Marsh Fritillary of Britain are examples. Larvae of the Milbert's Tortoise Shell live together when they are small, protected by a silken web, but they are inclined to split up and become more or less solitary when they are larger and require a greater bulk of food. A number of species of gregarious caterpillars protect themselves by weaving a web or tent for the group to shelter in.

For its size, a caterpillar consumes a lot of vegetation and, if the weather is mild, will grow surprisingly quickly. Because its skin is non-stretchable, the caterpillar must periodically shed its old skin for a new and larger one. Some species recycle the nutrients in the old skin by eating it, but others just move away and leave it where it is. I have occasionally come across a site used by a brood of Mourning Cloak caterpillars where the massed skin cases of a couple of different instars of these gregarious creatures could be seen among the branches. "Instar" is the name scientists use for the form or stage of an insect between moults; for instance, "second instar larva" means a larva in its second stage. The caterpillars of most butterflies pass through four or five instars, but some species have more, some less.

Butterflies that lay their eggs singly, normally spread them well out over the host plant or use a number of plants. Unless several females lay on the same plant, there are usually not sufficient caterpillars to do lasting harm to it. A healthy, well-growing row of parsnip, carrots, parsley, or celery in the vegetable garden can, for instance, play host to a surprising number of Short Tailed Swallowtail caterpillars without lessening the culinary value of the crop. Female butterflies seem to know or sense when there is another egg already in place on a leaf, and deliberately avoid it. This is not always so, of course, but I have been given this impression on a number of occasions when I was watching the behaviour of Swallowtails and Red Admirals. The Red Admiral also seems to avoid the leaves of nettles and to oviposit in the flower head if caterpillars of other species, especially gregarious ones, are already working the main body of the plant.

Many different types of predators include butterfly caterpillars in their diets; indeed, if it were not for predators and other natural controls, we would soon find our green world in a very serious situation. Nevertheless, there are times when I wish these natural controls were not quite so efficient. Where I live, for instance, butterfly populations are so low that one sometimes wonders, Why bother? Our harsh weather is undoubtedly the main cause of our problem, and since we now appear to be in an extended cycle of even worse weather, I expect our butterflies to become even more limited.

Caterpillars have developed a variety of protective characteristics in the course of their evolution that account for their species survival. Many have a colouration or form that is extremely difficult to see. Others have colours so bright and noticeable they are believed to serve as a scaring mechanism. Of the former, those of the Blues, the Sulphurs and the Small White butterfly are at times extremely difficult to locate. The caterpillars of some Swallowtails, like those of the Monarch butterfly, are said to have bitter body juices. Because distasteful caterpillars are brightly marked, birds preying on them quickly learn how unpleasant they taste and thereafter leave them strictly alone. The Tiger Swallowtail caterpillar has a large pair of orange, black-pupilled eyespots on the metathorax, the third segment back from the head, that is believed by some to serve either as a scaring mechanism or as a target to direct a bird's peck away from the vulnerable head. I incline against the latter idea, for surely a well-directed peck in this area would be equally harmful. Caterpillars of the Swallowtail family have the ability when disturbed to protrude quickly an orange, V-shaped scent organ or "osmeterium" and emit a sweet, cloying, pineapple-type scent that is also said to deter predators.

The silken webs spun by caterpillars are, of course, a form of protection; so is the tent of folded leaves made by the Red Admiral caterpillars. The spines on some types of caterpillars may be a deterrent to birds, but I often wonder just how effective they really are. Spines might deter a kinglet or a small warbler, but not a larger bird such as a jay or a crow. Certainly pheasants in Britain are reputed to be very fond of the caterpillars of the Heath Fritillary where both occur together. Heath Fritillaries have only small spines.

Some gregarious caterpillars have yet another type of defensive behaviour. If disturbed, a high percentage of the group will suddenly start moving simultaneously in a series of short, quick jerks. I have seen caterpillars of the Mourning Cloak or Camberwell Beauty do this on numerous occasions. Nor is this behaviour restricted to butterfly caterpillars; the larvae of the mountain ash sawfly do this also.

Some species find protection as a kind of spin-off from a symbiotic relationship with other insects. For example, ants will prey on the juvenile stage of certain other insects, yet they are very sociable towards the small, slug-like caterpillars of some species of Blue butterflies. They covet the honeydew secreted by the caterpillars and, by their presence, protect the caterpillars from other small predators such as spiders. I have seen ants in attendance on both the Spring Azure and the Silvery Blue butterflies. It is now well known how significant was a certain species of ant to the welfare of the Large Blue of Britain, but unfortunately the discovery was made too late to prevent the butterfly from becoming extinct there. I shall say more on this relationship later, in the chapter on conservation.

**The Pupa or Chrysalis** The radical change a caterpillar has to undergo to become an adult butterfly occurs during the stage known as the pupa or chrysalis. This is the resting stage, in which the amazing breakdown and reassembly of the caterpillar's body fluids and tissues into those of an adult butterfly take place. During this period the chrysalis neither eats, drinks, nor moves from place to place. In preparation for its change into a chrysalis, the caterpillar, when large enough, stops feeding, finds a suitable place to pupate, and then enters into a period of quiescence or inactivity. At the end of this period, which is usually about three days long, the caterpillar moults into a chrysalis. The chrysalis is actually formed within the caterpillar's skin. When this change is completed, the skin splits open, shrivels up and drops off from the tail-end of the newly-formed chrysalis. As with the egg and the caterpillar, the shape, size and colour of the chrysalis are determined by the butterfly family to which it belongs. A knowledgeable person in this field will be able to identify any individual specimen, certainly down to the family level.

Some caterpillars pupate loose on the ground, some fasten themselves to their host plant, and some roam from their rearing site and seek out a more secluded spot on which to attach themselves. Such sites can include the leeward side of a fence post, the crevices of a dry-stone wall, the inside of the garden shed, the back of a piece of loose bark, the interior of an abandoned car, and numerous other similarly sheltered spots.

For those chrysalids that attach themselves to something, the way in which they are attached indicates the butterfly family to which they belong. Many if not all of the Nymphalids, for instance, hang freely upside down by the tail-end. They stick to the substrate on a small pad of silk spun by the caterpillar, and grip it by means of a set of special hooks at the end of the abdomen called the "cremaster." Possibly this is the most common type of butterfly chrysalis the average person encounters. The Painted Lady, a Nymphalid, is a good example of a free-hanging chrysalis; indeed, its caterpillars can be quite creative in preparing a spot in which to hang up. They will occasionally construct a net from which to suspend themselves. The finest example of this I have seen was in mid-August of 1979. My wife had planted a few annual flowers among her vegetables in order to encourage bees and other pollinators to forage around the crops. A Painted Lady had oviposited on some viper's bugloss, but the full-grown caterpillars left the plant when the time came to pupate. One caterpillar pulled the two outer edges of a cucumber leaf towards each other, fastened them with silk, and then across the intervening gap built a silken net platform from which it suspended itself head down into this U-shaped vegetable shelter. The net was quite intricate and appeared perfectly level.

Not all caterpillars that attach themselves to something do so head down. Though all of them do indeed fasten their tail-end onto a tiny pad of silk by the cremaster, some, the Swallowtails and the Orange Tip of Britain for instance, position themselves head upwards. To do this, they must, of course, have some way to combat gravity, so in addition to firmly fastening their tail-ends, they weave a silken girdle around their middles, and attach it to their chosen resting places very much in the manner the electrical linesmen or professional tree climbers attach a safety belt when they are working up a pole or tree.

A butterfly at this stage of its life cycle is particularly vulnerable. Fortunately, the varied colouration and shapes of the different species afford the pupae a certain amount of protection by blending in with their general surroundings. Some butterflies, the Tiger and the Short Tailed Swallowtails for instance, produce two different colours of chrysalis, one a basic brown and the other greenish, and these are nearly always found on correspondingly coloured backgrounds. How they are programmed to blend in with the surroundings I cannot say. It may be the result of the host plant type or of climatic conditions during their caterpillar stage, or we may simply be seeing two different genetic strains. Anyway, it is very noticeable when these caterpillars are reared in captivity.

Not all species spend equal amounts of time as chrysalids. Presumably the sooner the adult butterfly emerges and takes flight, the less hazardous this stage is. Some species, our Spring Azure, the Holly Blue of Britain, and the Swallowtails, for instance, pass the whole winter in this stage, whereas certain others, the Painted Lady, the Small White, the White Admiral and the Mourning Cloak, for instance, may spend as little as sixteen days or less in this third stage of their development. The length of time a butterfly spends as a chrysalis depends to some extent on the prevailing humidity and air temperature. This seems particularly true for those species that normally spend only a short time in the chrysalis stage. Weather and emergence from the egg late in the season, may cause a species that usually overwinters as an adult to overwinter as a chrysalis instead.

It is often possible to see the adult butterfly's colours through the chrysalis wall shortly before it emerges. Captive Red Admirals are good ones to observe. The emergence of the full-grown butterfly from its tiny container is one of the wonders of nature. The wings are at first wet, and all crumpled up in a tight mass, but immediately on emergence they start to fall loose. The butterfly then pumps fluid from its body into the veins of its wings until they are fully extended. It then rests motionless with its wings held slightly apart, until they have dried and are ready for use in flight. Quite soon after taking flight the butterfly releases its body wastes from the anus as a droplet of red, "chalky" fluid, called "meconium." It is this waste matter that, released more or less simultaneously by large numbers of recently emerged butterflies, has given rise to the mythical showers of blood found in folklore. I have never been fortunate enough to see such an extraordinary congregation of emerging butterflies.

**The Imago or Adult Butterfly** There are roughly 20 000 recorded species of butterfly on earth. Of these, 695 are known in North America, with about 272 recognized in Canada. Britain has recorded only 64 species, while Newfoundland has even fewer, with 51. As a Canadian, I find it exciting that the experts believe there are still around 60 species yet to be discovered or recorded within Canada.

The possibility of the ordinary butterfly gardener's discovering a new species is rather slim. If there are any new species out there, I would expect them to be very similar to known species, differing only minimally from them and requiring a specialist in the particular family to distinguish them. On the other hand, the sighting of a species not yet recorded in your own particular area is entirely possible. If a new butterfly enters your area, there is a very good chance it will first be seen among the nectar-bearing flowers of a park or garden. It is likely that the recording will be made by a serious amateur. Double checking any doubtful butterfly that enters your garden goes hand in hand with good butterfly gardening. I have been fortunate in recording three new butterflies for Newfoundland and another one for my district simply by checking and double checking all the butterflies I see. A friend, who is actually more interested in birds than in butterflies, also recorded a new species for Newfoundland. He was taking a few coloured photographs in his garden, when he noticed what he described as "a rather pretty butterfly" feeding on showy sedum in the company of a Red Admiral. Since the light was just right and the butterfly extremely tame, he was able to take a number of good close-up photographs of it. We identified it as an almost perfect specimen of the Question Mark butterfly, and later had our identification verified by a Canadian expert. The point is that any observant person with a serious interest in natural history and gardening can make very worthwhile contributions. These might not be anything as spectacular as the recording of a new species, but they might be valuable nonetheless – for example, a sighting that extends the known range of a distinctive, easily recognized butterfly.

Not all species of butterfly are on the wing at the same time. Each species has its own time of the year when it can be encountered, and though the flight periods of some species do indeed overlap, there are others that could never under normal circumstances be seen on the wing together. This is particularly true in northern areas such as my own, where many species of butterfly have only one generation a year. Here, for instance, it would be most unlikely to encounter a Brown Elfin and a Pink Edged Sulphur together, for the former appears in April or May and the latter in July. Butterflies that overwinter as adults will be on the wing with a greater variety of other kinds than those that do not; they appear on the wing in the late summer and autumn and then again in the spring, and so mingle with both those that fly only in the late summer and autumn and those that fly only in the spring.

Nor do all butterflies have the same life expectancy. Butterflies that do not overwinter as adults probably live as adults for only a couple of weeks, but the overwintering species such as the Green Comma, the Milbert's Tortoise Shell and the Mourning Cloak will often survive for around ten months. Much of this time, of course, the butterflies spend in a torpid state, and not in physically wearing activities. The life expectancy of a butterfly depends to a great extent on the prevailing weather conditions, on the presence or absence of a variety of predators and parasites, and on the availability of suitable nectar. Most likely, those butterflies living in or adjacent to parks or gardens where an abundance and a variety of nectar are continually available, will live longer than those that do not.

Though the two sexes are almost identical in appearance in the Swallowtails and many other species, there are species in which the males and females are coloured or marked differently. This variation makes the identification of butterflies a little more troublesome for the beginner. Among this latter group are the Bog Copper of North America and the Common Blue of Britain. In some species, the Arctic or Checkered Skipper for instance, the female is slightly larger than the male; but this difference is really noticeable only when both sexes are viewed together, while they are coupled in mating for example. In some species, one sex may for a short period be on the wing before the other appears. If you happen to be out and about during this couple of days, you might find this a source of some confusion.

The butterfly is the climax of the four-stage metamorphosis I have described. It is this beautiful creature that most of us are primarily interested in, and that is the subject of the rest of this book.

*Overleaf:*
*The life cycle of the Short Tailed Swallowtail, shown here in a typical local habitat. This butterfly prefers the seashore and offshore islands where its favourite host plant grows, the scotch lovage (*Ligusticum scoticum*) shown here. It is somewhat choosy about nectar sources, but in season it can be seen nectaring from such native flowers as the Labrador tea (*Ledum groenlandicum*) shown here.*

# Butterfly Habitats

The butterfly's natural home, where it lives and goes about its everyday life, is termed its habitat. Generally speaking, except in the centre of the Sahara Desert or some such spot, there are many different types of habitat within reasonable distance of one other. Each of these habitats or environments will have its own characteristic plants and animals. For a habitat to be of any use to butterflies, it must be able to provide what is essential for sustaining butterfly life. This sounds obvious, but the matter is not quite as straightforward as it appears. Some habitats, a tidal pool for instance, are completely alien to butterflies, and others that appear ideal, attract no butterflies. In Newfoundland, for instance, there are only a few bogs that support the Dorcas Copper butterfly. Even though there are hundreds of other apparently identical bogs available, not a single individual is on them. Many factors, some of them quite obscure, must dictate whether or not a butterfly can inhabit an area. The two essential requirements are food for the caterpillars and suitable nectar-producing flowers for the adults. Regardless of other important things, if you know what plants satisfy these two basic requirements for each type of butterfly and where they occur, you can go out into the countryside to look for butterflies with a reasonable assurance of finding some.

In most untouched and near-natural areas there is often no easily discernible boundary between one habitat and another. More often than not, the vegetation changes gradually. In an area dominated by humans, however, this is not usually so; the boundary between, say, a grass meadow and a managed woodlot may be quite abrupt. Definite boundaries of this kind between habitats are more often seen in the highly manipulated countryside of a nation such as Britain than they are in my part of Canada.

In a more natural setting, where one habitat gives way to another gradually, there will usually occur a mixing of the wildlife of both habitats. Here, where two or more edge zones come together, there is often a very rich variety of wildlife because the whole mixed edge zone embraces something of each habitat and is therefore much more diversified. I am convinced that the creation of habitat diversity plays a large part in the successful encouragement of wildlife, particularly butterflies, in suburban areas and in other human-dominated environments.

This piece of ecological knowledge is well worth bearing in mind whenever you set out into the countryside to look for butterflies. Remember, however, that though a greater variety of butterflies may often be found in these mixed edge zones, a larger population of a particular species will be found in the specific habitat that most satisfies the essential requirements of that species. Large blocks of natural habitat such as a North American peat bog or an English chalk grassland, especially support large populations of a species. A mosaic of smaller habitats in a manipulated landscape, on the other hand, is less likely to support as large a population. Obviously, a small block of specialized habitat cannot be expected to hold as many special butterflies as one will find in a similar area ten times its size. Also, butterflies are more likely to move back and forth among small adjacent habitats simply because of the shorter distances involved, as long as these smaller habitats are not cut off from each other by impenetrable barriers such as tall trees.

In a city or suburban area, the gardens, parks, cemeteries, playing fields, abandoned building sites and numerous rough, neglected corners create a mixture of habitats. Butterflies will travel from one site to another, provided that the intervening inhospitable areas are not too large, nor the buildings too high or close together. Though the butterflies associated with such sites are normally only the commoner, more adaptable species, it is still good to know that these habitats are all playing a part in butterfly conservation.

Similar habitats in widely separated geographical locations will not necessarily host identical butterfly populations. Though some species, particularly widely distributed ones such as the Painted Lady and the Red Admiral, may be the same in habitats remote from one another, in general there will be some definite differences in the makeup of the butterfly fauna. A number of factors other than vegetation determine what butterfly will be found where; some of these are geology, altitude, climate and geographic location.

What follows is a brief description of some of the more common and obvious habitats, and of a few of the butterflies that populate them.

**Woodlands** The nature of a woodland is governed by the species, mix, density and age of the trees that grow in it, and of the smaller plants, if any, beneath them. Here in Newfoundland the vast stands of coniferous forest are made up of densely-growing black or white spruce and balsam fir. These forests are inhospitable to butterflies except where the sun gains access and where a variety of herbaceous vegetation is present. Hospitable sites can be found, but only in natural clearings such as where the trees have been felled by wind, or in artificial clearings such as along logging roads. Deciduous woodlands harbour much more wildlife, but in the Boreal Forest Zone most of the trees are conifers. Unfortunately for butterflies and for wildlife in general, softwood conifers are economically more valuable to us. It is sad to see how in Britain, for instance, the few great oaks and beeches remaining are rapidly disappearing, only to be replaced by regimented blocks of the faster-growing conifers. Thirty-odd years ago, when I was a gamekeeper there, the systematic destruction of the countryside was hardly underway. Woods were filled with primroses, violets, bluebells and lily-of-the-valley. When the wood anemone bloomed in the young plantations, it was as if the ground were covered with a quilt of fresh, fluffy snow. This cover has now been replaced by a thick mat of useless pine needles, and by thin, scraggly bracken groping for the sun. The nightingales and grasshopper warblers have disappeared, along with the blackthorn and other scrub. There are a few butterflies left along the wide rides, but none compared with what there used to be. For all that can be said against them, the old private game reserves and the practice of game bird shooting did make for the protection of wildlife.

One of the richest woodland habitats is created when the coniferous forest is destroyed by wildfire or by lumbering. It is then that pioneer plants such as aspen, fire cherry, wild raisin, raspberry and fireweed spring up to dominate the site. This young, fresh, deciduous scrub is beloved by Tiger Swallowtails, Pink Edged Sulphurs, White Admirals, and the Spring Azure in Newfoundland. As the trees and shrubs grow taller, these species are joined by the Mourning Cloak and the Compton Tortoise Shell.

These pioneer plants almost invariably spring up on any piece of disturbed land adjacent to the coniferous forest. Their abundance has given Newfoundland long ribbons of this type of habitat along both sides of the rural roadways and the main highway across the island. I believe the scrub is a definite advantage to our butterfly population, especially when it is interspersed with grassy areas that enable Ringlets and Skippers to thrive there.

Pioneer plant species vary with geographical location, but they are undoubtedly equally important to the butterflies of every region. Incidentally, this type of habitat can be readily duplicated by the butterfly gardener on either side of the Atlantic. By selecting the plants representative of this type of habitat in your own region, you can make a very useful addition to the overall plan of a backyard butterfly sanctuary.

In their natural setting, pioneer plants will gradually be replaced. Over many years the habitat will move through a number of stages, until once again the primeval species of trees become completely dominant. This is the "climax forest." Each stage in the succession will prove most beneficial to a different insect fauna. Indeed, as the habitat changes, so too will its fauna. The butterfly gardener who knows what stage in the succession each forest butterfly requires, can favour any desired species by maintaining the vegetation at the stage of development that species prefers. Remember, however, that a climax forest may be the essential habitat for certain non-butterfly species – its destruction by anything other than natural means must be discouraged. But anyone fighting to reclaim a piece of damaged land and having an interest in attracting butterflies, can, to some degree, reconstruct forest or forest-associated habitats artificially, or arrest common habitat types at a desired stage of their development. This is by no means as simple or as straightforward as it may sound, however. The reconstruction or manipulation of natural habitats requires considerable skill. It also requires

*The very beautiful native rhodora (*Rhododendron canadense*) is extremely common along many of the roadsides in Newfoundland. It's a pity that this early-blooming and garden-worthy shrub attracts only the occasional Tiger Swallowtail, as shown here.*

considerable knowledge, which can be acquired only by long and painstaking research. There are some very competent and dedicated researchers, in both North America and Britain, diligently striving to unravel the problems of habitat management and so save our butterflies.

When you are devising a butterfly habitat to encompass the whole home garden, you could quite appropriately simulate a forest glade by planting deciduous shrubs and small trees of local pioneer species. You could even mix plants from a number of similar habitats and still create what is basically a woodland glade. By mixing, you could lay the foundation of a habitat for quite a large variety of butterflies. Though a garden of this nature can be sited some distance from a block of natural woodland, a sufficient number of them adjacent to one another can form a very good substitute for the real thing. In Newfoundland the Mourning Cloak will often lay its eggs on the willows or poplars in similar gardens. Other woodland butterflies such as the Green Comma, the Compton Tortoise Shell and, more recently, the White Admiral, will also occasionally visit these sites. Here, even in the capital city of St. John's, the forest is never very far away. Maybe the butterflies consider the local gardens simply edge zones or fringes of forest reaching outwards onto the land. Many municipal parks, even in heavily industrialized cities, may in a way never intended by the planners present the local butterflies with an imitation of a mixed-forest, forest-glade and edge-zone environment.

As with birds, not all forest butterfly species are found together in the forest, nor are they all active at the same elevation. From the forest floor up through the canopy and to the treetops, are several different living spaces. Each living space may meet certain specific requirements common to some but not all of the woodland butterflies. Furthermore, living spaces at different elevations may be attractive at different times of the year. The White Admiral butterfly, for instance, spends much of its time, after emerging from the chrysalis, well up in the forest canopy, but as the summer and fall flowers begin to appear, it spends an increasing amount of its time just above ground level searching for nectar. In North America at this time it is particularly fond of feeding from such flowers as pearly everlasting, bristly sarsaparilla, lance-leaved goldenrod, fireweed or willow herb, and the blooms of wild raspberry. A similar example, the Purple Hairstreak, a small butterfly associated with the oak forests of Britain, apparently spends most of its adult life high up in the canopy but sometimes descends in search of moisture or honeydew, a secretion of aphids. The time of day and the weather may also influence where a woodland butterfly will be. A bright, warm morning may, for instance, see the Tiger Swallowtail of North America fluttering and sailing well up among the middle canopy at the woodland's edge, but a very hot, dry afternoon may find the same butterfly down on the ground probing damp mud or even resting in the shade of the undergrowth.

Although the so-called forest butterflies may be dependent on the forest for food in their caterpillar stage, and for shelter, the adult must be able to find sufficient nectar. Generally, plants that are the greatest nectar producers require a considerable amount of moisture and sunlight and so must grow away from the trees. Unless a woodland is blessed with many large glades or is intersected by wide rides suitable for the growth of nectar-producing plants, the resident butterflies will have to leave the wood in order to search nearby meadows or other flower-bearing habitats. If these are not available, the woodland itself will have few butterflies.

**Bogs and Fens** In many parts of the world, especially in the north of the Soviet Union and Canada, there are large areas where the ground is always moist and the "soil" environment acidic. Here, dead plant matter has accumulated as peat in thick organic layers to create bogs and fens. To the expert there are many different types of bogs, but here, since we are dealing with them only in a superficial way, there is no need to go into their differences, which result from differences in geology, climate and geography. Fens too have their differences, but since they are, very generally speaking, just bogs with a different type of flora that results from the flow of water and additional nutrients through them, I shall consider them together with bogs. But if you are more than casually interested in these habitats, consult one of your local experts. Detailed environmental analysis requires special training and experience. Even a simple word such as "fen" may conjure up different images to different people. I am willing to bet that the term "fen" as used by a wildlife ecologist in Canada refers to a habitat quite different from the one referred to by a naturalist from, say, Cambridgeshire, England. Since I have no knowledge of the latter, I shall confine my remarks to the type of bogs and fens found throughout the Canadian Boreal Forest Zone.

In Newfoundland these environments are characterized by acid-loving plants such as pitcher plant, sundew, cranberry and sphagnum moss, and by the small shrubs, bog laurel, bog rosemary, sweet gale, leatherleaf and rhodora. Trees here are black spruce and larch, with the occasional alder. These sites also have a large and representative number of grasses and sedges.

The bog, at least in summer, is a beautiful environment, of great interest to the wildflower and butterfly enthusiast alike. Many bogs are extensively covered with a variety of orchids and other delicate wildflowers. Although some of these blooms are used as nectar sources, and the leaves of some bog-loving shrubs as ovipositing or sunning sites, it is more often the grasses that are most attractive to bogland butterflies.

Butterflies using this habitat are relatively few. The most characteristic bogland butterflies in my own part of Canada are the Jutta Arctic, the Bog Copper, the Dorcas Copper and, to some extent, the Northern Blue and the Arctic or Checkered Skipper. These last two species are also found elsewhere; since bogland often adjoins forest or heathland, there is a mixing of species typical of these habitats. The Inornate Ringlet, a butterfly of meadowland and other drier, grassy areas, can often, for instance, be found on bogland in small numbers. Also, I have seen a Short Tailed Swallowtail, not normally a bogland butterfly, imbibing nectar from the flowers of the bog candle orchid, *Habenaria dilatata*. In Britain, where the wet-ground habitats are disappearing at an alarming rate as a result of artificial draining, only a very few butterflies are associated with these habitats. The English Swallowtail, the Small Mountain Ringlet and the Dutch race of the Large Copper – these are associated with damp environments, and sadly, all are rare and exceedingly localized butterflies.

The wet environments on both sides of the Atlantic have many of the same or quite similar plant species associated with them, but on the whole the two environments are different. In much of Britain, these habitats, along with the lakes, ponds, rivers and streams, are far less acidic and more nutrient-rich than are the aquatic and wet-ground habitats of Newfoundland.

Though the occasional bogland butterfly may by chance appear in a butterfly garden sited in the countryside, there is normally not much point in deliberately trying to attract them. For the average person the environment would be very difficult and expensive to recreate. It would be more appropriate to visit the natural habitat of these butterflies in order to enjoy them.

**Seashore** The seashore, that area of land between the high tide mark and the salt water, is naturally devoid of breeding butterflies. But though there is no insect that can actually live in the sea, the coastal strip of land just above and inland from the high tide mark is a very different matter. Habitats along a length of coastline can vary considerably. In Newfoundland, for instance, such habitats can range from huge, towering cliffs to soft, rolling sand dunes. Sometimes even the forest will be found growing right down to the high tide mark, even on exposed coastlines. Here, however, the trees are usually small, stunted spruce of little if any value to butterflies. On the other hand, in the sheltered coves and bays the tree growth will actually hang over the water's edge at high tide, and will not be made up solely of spruce and fir but will contain a sprinkling of birch, mountain maple, dogberry and the like. Here we can sometimes see woodland butterflies in this generally inhospitable edge zone. I have seen our uncommon Compton Tortoise Shell perched on a tree trunk, wings open, sunning itself in such a site. Our White Admiral can quite often be seen patrolling the water's edge, occasionally alighting on the wet sand and seaweed or taking short exploratory flights over the salt water.

Like any other habitat, the coastal strip has its own specialized flora, but this is often mixed with other, more common, vegetation, depending on the habitat that backs onto it. Two plants intimately associated with the seashore in Newfoundland are the scotch lovage and the beach or sea pea. Here, but not necessarily elsewhere, these species are, respectively, the favourite host plants of the Short Tailed Swallowtail and the Silvery Blue butterflies. The Short Tailed Swallowtail can also be found in other habitats, but in Newfoundland its favourite habitat is undoubtedly the coastline and offshore islands where scotch lovage abounds. Indeed, on occasion this butterfly can be encountered by the hundreds in these locations. It is, however, rarely seen along stretches of coastline where the scotch lovage is absent. This plant thrives especially where the ground is kept rich with seabird droppings. But it is easily propagated from seed, and survives well enough in my rock garden, where I have counted as many as thirteen larvae on a single plant.

In some areas of North America the Silvery Blue is common and widely distributed, and inhabits open woodlands and meadows. In Newfoundland, however, it appears to be tied solely to the relatively few stretches of coastline where the beach or sea pea flourishes. Indeed, I have found that this small butterfly rarely ventures very far away from patches of this pea. If hard pressed it may fly off in a wide arc, but it soon returns to the general area from which it was flushed. This beautiful little butterfly also seems to have a very limited number of flower types from which it seeks nectar. I have never seen one nectaring from anything other than beach pea – it is true, of course, that even in a favourable site very few other nectar producers grow close to this species. This example illustrates rather nicely how some butterflies are tied to just a few types, perhaps only one type, of plant or habitat – unfortunately so, in these times of rampant habitat destruction. One of the most infamous examples of a species too closely tied to a specialized environment is the Xerces Blue of California. In 1943 an expanding military facility destroyed the habitat of the only colony left in existence, and so another beautiful species disappeared forever.

The seashore or coastline also acts as a travel route and landfall area for migrating butterflies. This is said to be particularly noticeable along the south coast of England. My friends tell me that here, at the right time, large numbers of Clouded Yellow and Painted Lady butterflies can readily be seen and enjoyed as they come in from the Continent and settle down to refuel from the local flowers. It is fortunate that wildflowers rich in nectar are often abundant along the clifftop meadows and crumbling banksides of such a coastline. They are a very important feature of this habitat because they succour the tired, incoming butterflies and so prepare them for the next step in their journey – with luck, inland to your garden! I have never heard of large groups of butterflies being seen entering Newfoundland. Small groups of a dozen or so have been seen – I have come across tired, newly-arrived Painted Lady butterflies feeding from the flowers of Labrador tea, and Monarchs feeding from red clover – but they are by no means common. One of our problems in Newfoundland is that our island is so vast, and has so much territory inaccessible except by bush plane or helicopter, that we are really only beginning to know what is going on here in the butterfly world.

**Heath and Moorland** Because they support no timber, heathlands in Newfoundland are referred to as "barrens." They are open, windswept, almost treeless areas blanketed over with a covering of ericaceous shrubs such as blueberry, Labrador tea, sheep laurel and mountain cranberry – and so definitely not barren. On the higher ground the plant types are dwarfed and more mat-forming, and plants such as sheep laurel give way to tundra bilberry, mountain avens, alpine azaleas and diapensia.

There are usually a lot of boulders on the surface, and often there are areas of exposed earth, in these sites, especially on the higher ground, where the wind and frost have great effect. The ground is stony and nutrient-poor. Many of these bare patches form slight depressions among the surrounding vegetation and so provide suitable sunning areas for the local butterflies. Often a fair quantity of native grass and sedge grows among the heathland plants or forms separate small habitats spotting the entire heathland or barrens. All these features add diversity and so increase variety in the butterflies and other small wildlife that can inhabit the heathland.

Butterflies typical of this habitat in Newfoundland are the Brown Elfin and the Northern Blue. On the higher ground the Arctic Blue and the Pelidne Sulphur make an appearance, the former often in large numbers. Because the dips, valleys and hollows of heathlands often contain small lakes, ponds, or streams, and, of course, patches of bog and tree scrub, certain non-typical heathland butterflies will sometimes be seen there. The Tiger Swallowtail, the Jutta Arctic and the Inornate Ringlet are three such butterflies.

One never knows for sure what may turn up in any given habitat. I remember once being taken by small helicopter to one of Newfoundland's most barren serpentine hilltops. Plant life of any sort is extremely scarce at this site, and the vast expanse of bare red-brown rock gives one a good impression of what the surface of the moon must look like. Though it was a warm, beautifully calm, sunny day, I did not expect to see any butterflies in this inhospitable place. But to my surprise a number of Short Tailed Swallowtails were fluttering around. There certainly did not appear to be anything there to attract them, yet there they were, well away from the type of countryside that is considered normal for them. Thinking back over the incident, I am inclined to believe that they were engaged in what is referred to as "hilltopping." The reasons for hilltopping are still open to speculation, but it is possible that butterflies of certain species use the technique of coming together from over a large territory and congregating atop a prominent natural landmark as a sure means of locating and acquiring a mate.

The heath or moorland of Britain is quite different from that of Newfoundland, with the most obvious difference being the preponderance there of heather, bracken fern and gorse. Also, the British growing season is longer and the weather milder and less windy. Unfortunately, Britain is losing a great deal of this type of habitat as a result of the techniques of modern farming and forestry, the expansion of towns and villages, and the construction of super-highways. Canada has its own development, but with its vast expanses of land in reserve, it is not yet, as far as I know, losing any of its more widespread butterflies. In Canada, some local populations have undoubtedly been depleted or forced farther back into the wilderness, but in Britain many butterfly species are now extremely rare.

Two declining species of the British heathland are the Grayling and the Silver Studded Blue. The Grayling in particular shows a marked affinity for the seacoast, and there I still see the odd one on my occasional visits home. This butterfly seems to enjoy settling on a weathered rock or patch of bare earth. The Brown Elfin of Newfoundland also spends a considerable amount of its time resting on bare earth, especially in a sun-warmed depression.

On the whole, there are not many butterflies associated with heath or moorland. It is a rugged environment. Owing to the incessant wind, our heathland species spend their brief lives within 1 metre (3 feet) of the ground. The tiny ones such as the Brown Elfin and the Arctic Blue are difficult to locate, as they flutter and zig-zag among the low-growing plants and the boulders. Heathland species have become adapted to gathering their nectar upside down, no doubt because so many of the nectar producers of this environment have evolved inverted urn-shaped flowers that trap the

*The small cranberry, or marshberry as it is called in Newfoundland, provides nectar for the tiny Arctic Blue. Flying low to the ground, this is a fairly common though rarely noticed July butterfly of our hilltops and coastal barrens. The plant is also the host of another tiny North American butterfly, the Bog Copper.*

warmth of the sun and produce nectar despite the cool winds that whistle over them.

A serious and all too frequent hazard to the heath or moorland habitat, caused by humans, is fire. Over the years I have seen some terrible fires burning out of control, both in Britain and in Canada. The effect on the butterfly populations, as on wildlife in general, must be phenomenal, and is impossible to assess. Many of these fires are caused by careless or indifferent picnickers who have no inkling of the consequences of their actions. A moose or hare breaking cover with its fur on fire, or a ptarmigan cooked on its nest, is a shattering sight.

**Meadows and Pasture** My part of Canada is not blessed with an abundance of farmland. Newfoundland is more a land of fishing villages and vast expanses of wilderness than of agricultural communities. Even so, we do have a few pockets of farmland, where rough meadowland has been wrested from the forest and from which a thin but sweet-smelling crop of hay is gathered annually. Also, around the coastline, with its scattered fishing outports, there is the odd tiny meadow where a handful of sheep, the family cow and a single work pony graze, stoically ignoring the North Atlantic storms. Often these small meadows are filled with wildflowers. Buttercups, hawkweeds, red and white clovers, ox-eye daisies, asters and goldenrods abound, and in the damper, somewhat richer sites, lady's smocks or cuckoo flowers, bog candles and five or six species of orchid. They remind me of British meadows thirty-odd years ago. Nowadays, however, British farming, with its "improved" seed mixes, chemical fertilizers, herbicides and burning stubbles, does not initiate meadow environments that favour wildlife. I am told that rarely now can cows be seen standing belly-deep in buttercups, or a brood of partridge be watched sunning on a flattened molehill. Modern farming there has systematically extracted much of the goodness of the land without due consideration for tomorrow.

There are several different types of grassland, ranging from the natural to the human-made. They are usually significantly different in their botanical makeup. Natural or ancient meadows will usually have a very varied and intricately balanced plant association, whereas in human-made pastureland the ground will be covered with a thick turf of dominant grass species, planted and nurtured by the farmer. A pasture is usually part of the farm's crop rotation and so is not as stable as a meadow. These differences between the two types of grassland will influence the variety and number of butterflies and other insects that establish populations in them. The British Nature Conservancy Council stated in *The Conservation of Butterflies* in 1981 that "whereas natural grassland may support 20 species of butterfly, artificial improved grassland supports none"!

The soil on which a meadow is growing, also, of course, has a significant bearing on what plants and butterflies are present. So too does the presence or absence of grazing animals, wild or domestic. Generally speaking, a meadow established on shallow, impoverished soil produces a greater variety of grasses and wildflowers than does a pasture on deep, rich loam – this is an extremely significant point for the butterfly gardener or butterfly reserve manager to bear in mind, no matter what the location.

Grazing animals can be either detrimental or beneficial to grassland butterflies, depending on the species of grazer and the time of year the grazing is done. This applies not only in intensively cultivated countries such as Britain, but also in those areas of North America where herds of wild or domestic animals depend on grasses or other ground vegetation for food. In marginal grasslands particularly, grazing animals will assist in stopping the encroachment and eventual takeover of meadows by scrub. A fine example could once be seen in the south of England. Before the autumn of 1953, when myxomatosis, a virus disease of rabbits, was introduced, rabbits grazed the chalk downs and helped to maintain the typical chalkland flora by stopping the encroaching scrub from growing up and smothering the grasses and wildflowers. These downs were a mecca for butterflies, particularly some of the Blues. But now that the rabbits are depleted, the scrub is rapidly gaining dominance, and this prime butterfly habitat is disappearing. Nature reserve officers are experimenting with various domestic animals and with techniques such as mowing, to find a suitable alternative to grazing by rabbits. Maintaining grass at a suitable height for butterflies is not as easy as it may appear. Not all grazing animals feed or crop the grass in the same way. Not all butterfly species flourish in grass of the same length. In Britain, for instance, the Lulworth Skipper and the Marbled White require long grass, the Silver Spotted Skipper and the Adonis Blue, short. It may be that both long and short grass can be maintained adjacent to each other, by fencing off blocks of grass within the main grazing areas or, on a small scale, by having tethered ponies or calves graze. Either method would allow a desirable mosaic of short and long turf to be created. Cattle are generally considered better than sheep for grassland management because they do not crop the grass so short. Rabbits, though they crop grass short, are an improvement over sheep, because they are far better at controlling young trees and scrub that invade the meadow and because they do not compact the ground as badly as sheep. Goats could prove useful for controlling scrub, but as most people know, they have the nasty habit of destroying anything edible and within reach! Meadow management for the benefit of butterflies is a difficult, complicated business. Animals grazing at the wrong time of year could, for instance, destroy a lot of butterfly eggs or larvae. In mild climates such as Britain's, winter grazing may prove the least damaging, but in North America much of the ground at this time of year is under a deep covering of snow. Mowing is generally considered a poor substitute for grazing, but it may yet prove the only feasible alternative in some situations. In North America, prescribed burning is used to manage remnants of native prairie. Done properly it certainly benefits the indigenous flora, but despite all the reassurances that it is not detrimental to the associated insect fauna, including butterlies, I am not yet convinced of its harmlessness. In the rotational burning of small blocks within a larger area, the burnt ground will be repopulated by insects from the surrounding habitats, but surely this rule does not necessarily hold for the burning of areas of vast extent, such as a prairie or heather moorland. I believe that the practice of using fire as a management tool for butterflies requires considerable detailed research before it can be generally recommended.

*A somewhat idyllic impression of the British countryside during a happier ecological era. Before myxomatosis hit Britain, the myriad rabbits helped to maintain open grasslands by constantly nibbling down enroaching trees and shrubs. In suitable habitats their maintenance of the land encouraged the presence of wild thyme and of a particular species of ant. The Large Blue butterfly, shown in the bottom right corner, was dependent on both the thyme and the ant, and is now extinct. Note the ant carrying the Blue's caterpillar home to its nest – such was the symbiotic relationship between these two creatures. The simply-coloured but strikingly beautiful Marbled Whites nectaring above the Large Blues, increase an exile's nostalgia for summer days long past.*

The depth of the water table and the wetness of the soil also influence the type of vegetation and butterflies to be found in meadows. Dry-meadow butterflies here include the Inornate and the McIsaac's Ringlets, the Clouded Sulphur, the Painted Lady, the Red Admiral and the European or Essex Skipper. Moist meadows, as well as damp woodland edges and glades, are inhabited by the Atlantis and the Silver Bordered Fritillaries, the Pearl Crescent and, to some extent, the Arctic or Checkered Skipper.

As I have mentioned, the meadows in my part of the world are small and usually intermixed with woodland or scrub. We can therefore often see woodland butterflies mingling with meadow butterflies. In many other parts of Canada and the United States, there are vast, unmixed expanses of grassland or prairie, and these areas are inhabited by butterflies more closely tied to these specific environments.

Some of the commoner, more widespread meadow butterflies such as the Painted Lady and the Red Admiral can readily be attracted into the home garden if a suitable grassy area and related flora are provided for them, but far more species have requirements too peculiar to specific natural habitats. Sadly, our main concern must be whether or not they can remain in existence, rather than how to attract them into the home garden.

**Gardens and Suburban Areas** The world's increasing human population, with its demand for food, work and living space, puts an ever-growing burden on the natural countryside, especially on the land within commuting distance of population centres. Since natural habitats are extremely slow to regenerate and impossible to replace, the destructive effect on wildlife, compared to a human life span, is virtually permanent. Although some wildlife species such as the starlings and the grey squirrels have quickly adjusted to life within this new, human-dominated environment, others either have been forced to retreat to more compatible areas, where these are available, or, sadly, have become extinct.

But cities and towns need not be barren of wildlife; indeed, with sufficient space in suitably managed parks, gardens and greenbelts, a surprising quantity and diversity of wildlife can be encouraged and supported. Butterflies are no exception. Many butterflies, especially of the family *Nymphalidae*, appear quite at home in artificial environments. In one British garden not much bigger than a sixteenth of a hectare (an eighth of an acre) where considerable butterfly research has been done, 10 830 butterflies belonging to 21 species were marked and released during a six-year period. This, to me, seems remarkable, and makes me wish I had the time and human resources to do similar monitoring here. In Newfoundland, however, our gardens are still more or less cheek by jowl with natural countryside and so possibly would not have the same attraction for butterflies as does a well-planned garden in suburban Britain.

To be of value to butterflies, a habitat, whether artificial or natural, must have certain basic features. These include a reliable supply of nectar from the spring through the fall, plenty of suitable host plants, protection from widely destructive human agents and activities such as insecticides and burning, shelter from excessive winds, and exposure to as much sunshine as possible. Many older parks, gardens, churchyards and waste lots have these features and so have fortunately become attractive. Though it is very often a slow, tortuous business, nature will eventually reclaim even the most sordid urban site and give it some semblance of interest and beauty. Not many years ago a little piece of waste land in the east end of London, England, was found to harbour, among other things, doves, pheasants and fifteen species of butterflies.

It is too bad that so many modern municipal parks and private gardens are managed in a formal, sterile manner. Modern graveyards too, being still active, are usually kept like new pins, and so cannot compete with the old, abandoned resting places of our ancestors as habitats for butterflies. Most forms of wildlife abhor neatness and regimentation in the environment; such places, in comparison with more natural sites, are often biological barrens. If you happen to have a fetish for neatness and general tidying up, the odds are that you will not make a successful butterfly gardener. But it is still possible in beautiful gardens and parks to attract and maintain the smaller forms of wildlife such as butterflies, bumblebees, dragonflies, frogs and birds. Informal landscapes need not be horticultural slums, regardless of what some horticulturists and city planners believe.

There are, of course, innumerable habitats other than those briefly discussed in this chapter. The classification and study of natural environments is a highly complex discipline; if you are interested in having more information, speak with a local expert or read a more detailed text. One point to remember is that individual habitats may be either large or small. Generally speaking, the larger the block of any particular habitat, the better it is for the survival of those species, both plant and animal, that depend on it. On the other hand, a good-sized mosaic of smaller but different habitats will result in a much richer diversity of species than would any large monoculture. In trying to manage any butterfly or to attract a diversity of species, the nature reserve manager has a better chance of success than has the average home gardener, because the reserve manager has a greater area and variety of land with which to work. A gardener generally has to make do with creating a mixture of very small habitats in the hope that a variety of passing female butterflies will find one attractive and stay around long enough to oviposit. Such recreated habitats, however, may not individually be large enough to maintain viable populations. This is one of the reasons why the home garden butterfly enthusiast has to rely largely on the more wide-ranging or the migrating butterflies such as the *Nymphalidae*.

*Overleaf:*
*The destruction of butterfly habitat is a universal problem. Fortunately, many butterflies, if given half a chance, will adapt to human-made environments. Rough corners, city parks, derelict industrial sites, old churchyards and private gardens can all play a small role in the preservation of the world's butterfly fauna. Here, an old, somewhat neglected graveyard in Britain proves its value to these lovely insects. Moving upwards and across from left to right, we see the Small Tortoise Shell, the Brimstone, the Small White, the Holly Blue, the Peacock, the Comma and the Red Admiral – some of the most beautiful of garden butterflies.*

How large a specific habitat has to be before it can be of lasting value is debatable. For the average homeowner it may prove more appropriate to manage the garden as a pseudo–open glade in deciduous woodland, than to attempt to create one of the more specialized environments. Enough gardens of this kind, especially if adjacent to one another, would constitute a most valuable habitat for certain types of butterfly.

Knowing something about the natural habitat requirements of the individual local species of butterfly is useful for the butterfly gardener. Regardless of what I said in the last paragraph, if enough land is available the butterfly gardener should try to create several habitats – but this is, of course, easier said than done. If it is not possible, a little thought and effort can produce an artificial habitat that is a sort of conglomeration of some of the valuable features of a variety of natural environments. This "hodgepodge" habitat is often the best that many of us can manage. It is nice to know that it will attract many kinds of butterflies. Remember that though the term "habitat" used in reference to the countryside can mean a bog, a rough meadow, or a block of forest, in the home garden it can refer to an individual flower bed, a square metre or a few square feet of rough grass, or the damp ground surrounding a miniature pond. In working with butterflies in the home garden, one must of necessity think small.

# The Behaviour of Butterflies and General Ecology

**Migration** Unfortunately, there is far less known and understood about butterfly migration than about bird migration. One reason for this is that relatively few butterflies migrate whereas very many birds do. Also, birds make much easier subjects for research into migration, primarily because they are easier to mark for later identification and are more readily rediscovered at the end of their flight. On the whole, they also live longer. As every ornithologist knows, one of the biggest problems in studying migration in birds is the relatively small proportion of banded birds recaptured. The likelihood of rediscovering marked butterflies is decidedly less.

The most famous migratory butterfly is undoubtedly the Monarch of North America. This large, spectacular butterfly migrates northwards into Canada from Mexico or the southern United States each spring, and southwards again in the fall. It is unlikely that any individual remains alive long enough to undertake both north and south flights, though it has been suggested that some do. Though the Monarch is said to cover distances often in excess of 1900 km (1180 mi.) in only a few days, registering an average speed of 130 km (80 mi.) per day, most individuals probably do no better than 25–35 km (15–20 mi.) per day.

I have had very little personal experience with the Monarch because Newfoundland is too far east of its migration routes. A few, however, are reported here each year, and in September of 1973, the year of the phenomenal population increase of this butterfly in North America, many thousands were observed on our island. Indeed, there were clouds of several thousand reported flying past fishing boats 5 kilometres (3 miles) off our coastline. I once came across a small group feeding on a strip of red clover just above high tide mark in an abandoned settlement on our southern shore. They appeared exhausted, and rightly or wrongly I decided they had only very recently landed after crossing from the mainland. Happily, we do get the occasional Monarch sailing around the flower beds in the Botanical Garden and so far have recorded them nectaring on butterfly bush, goldenrod, cosmos and knapweed. These are probably butterflies that have been blown off course by particularly strong west or southwest winds. Newfoundland is the last possible landfall before Great Britain for a navigator disoriented in this way. Though many such butterflies must surely fall into the Atlantic, the occasional one does reach the British Isles, where the species is known as the Milkweed butterfly. In 1968 over 50 Monarch or Milkweed butterflies were recorded in southwest England, and in 1981 some 140 were reported from Britain.

Monarchs are not the only butterflies that migrate. In mainland North America other migratory butterflies include the Painted Lady, the American Painted Lady, the Buckeye, the Purple Wing, the Little Sulphur, the Cloudless Sulphur, the Great Southern White, the Question Mark, and possibly the Alfalfa and the Red Admiral. In Britain perhaps the best known migrants are the Painted Lady, the Red Admiral and the Clouded Yellow. These butterflies have been known to arrive in spectacular swarms from across the English Channel. Though their numbers are not as great as in the past, the sight can still stir the adrenalin.

In my own part of Canada the most obvious migrants are the two species of Painted Lady, and possibly the Alfalfa and the Red Admiral, believed to come in from the mainland. True to form, the two Painted Ladies do not appear every season, nor do they always appear in the same year as each other. The Painted Lady usually arrives from late May onwards and breeds extensively throughout Newfoundland, whereas the American Painted Lady usually does not arrive until September – which is, I believe, the reason it has rarely been recorded breeding. Certainly we have plenty of pearly everlasting (*Anaphalis margaritacea*), one of the potential host plants for this butterfly. Whether the new generation of our Painted Lady migrates southwards in the fall or just dies out is not certain. Some individuals definitely stay around too long and so perish, but many appear to move out well ahead of the winter weather. I have had dozens of recently emerged Painted Ladies suddenly disappear en masse from the flower beds when still only a couple of days old.

As I have said, it is impossible to offer an irrefutable solution to the riddle of butterfly migration. Some authorities believe that no individual butterflies travel the whole migration route but that the species accomplishes these long-distance movements by generation leapfrogging. Their theory is that the butterflies leave their wintering ground, advance northwards some distance, and then deposit eggs to give rise to another generation. This new generation then moves farther northwards, lays, and starts the whole process all over again. How many generations it takes for the species to make an appearance on its northern range, depends on such things as the speed of the spring's northward advance and the distance between the butterflies' original departure point and their final destination.

There are three types of butterfly migrants into Canada or Britain. First are those species that are only breeding visitors; second, those that are non-breeding visitors; and third, those that are normally recognized as being fully resident. Some migrants, such as the Red Admiral in Britain, may rarely overwinter in the new location but breed fairly regularly there, maintaining their continuous presence throughout the summer by annual immigration. Other species, such as the Mourning Cloak or Camberwell Beauty in Canada, may be permanent residents that overwinter with no problem but still have their population periodically boosted by the annual migration of their fellows from farther south. Yet others, such as the Question Mark in Newfoundland or the Monarch in Britain, appear only very occasionally, and never, as far as is known, manage to breed there. The occasional influx of Camberwell Beauties into Britain offers another such example. If by chance a few Camberwell Beauties arriving in Britain did manage to survive there until sexually mature the following spring, they would likely be so widely dispersed throughout the whole countryside that they would be unable to locate each other in time to breed.

Migration requires the expenditure of a lot of energy. Butterflies, like birds, create this energy by burning accumulated body fat. Also like birds, many butterflies feed along the way, and thus conserve their body fat and possibly extend their potential range. If you happen to have property on the flight lines of migrating butterflies, you can offer them considerable assistance by ensuring the availability of a plentiful supply and variety of nectar-bearing flowers in a warm, sheltered and sunny situation.

The actual physical appearance of a butterfly that has recently migrated into an area is often remarkably good. Indeed, they are often in so nearly perfect a condition one is tempted to believe that they are locally bred and only recently emerged from the chrysalis. The general belief that a migrant butterfly must be well worn is a fallacy. In fact, the wings of a butterfly are far more likely to get torn and the scales worn off during its everyday contact with local grass, bushes and predators than during its flight through long distances of sky. I have seen Monarchs and American Painted Ladies, both of which are suspected to breed at the most only rarely in Newfoundland, in such immaculate condition among the flower beds in the Botanical Garden that it was hard to believe such fragile-looking creatures had recently navigated such long distances.

Like me, you have probably wondered how migrating butterflies, or birds for that matter, can manage to find their way to wherever it is they are going. It is very tempting to put it all down to instinct and leave it at that, but is this so? Some researchers working with the Monarch now believe that this butterfly can find its way down to its wintering grounds because the upper part of its body contains a quantity of magnetite or magnetic iron oxide, the material that was once used in making compass needles. Since this substance is highly influenced by the earth's magnetic field, it may be that Monarchs are in effect carrying a built-in compass. Honeybees and homing pigeons also possess magnetite. There are other scientific explanations too, although these are too complicated to be outlined here.

It may be that groups of some resident breeding butterflies migrate southwards out of the home area. In Alberta, Canada, the Mourning Cloak or Camberwell Beauty has been recorded flying south among the migrating swarms of Monarchs. The Mourning Cloaks occasionally found in Britain are possibly individuals migrating southwards from Scandinavia. I have on occasion observed White Admiral and Compton Tortoise Shell butterflies fly southwards out to sea and quickly disappear from sight. Why these two resident breeding butterflies do this or where they are going, I don't know; I have always assumed they would find and alight on another peninsula, or do a wide swing back towards the spot they had just left, or eventually ditch in the sea and drown. My observations have always been of single specimens, never of groups.

Migrating butterflies, like birds, may sometimes be blown off course by hurricanes or even by minor storms. Unusual birds often appear in Newfoundland after inclement weather of this kind. Butterflies caught up in a thermal, or column of warm rising air, can reach a considerable height and so drift a considerable distance. It seems reasonable to assume that migrating butterflies soaring at high altitudes with a following wind, save considerable energy, especially over long distances. Indeed, soaring in this energy-saving way may be the norm for those butterflies that can travel long distances without feeding. As I mentioned earlier, it is more than likely that this is why the occasional Monarch turns up in England. Some people suggest that birds, butterflies and other insects discovered in places well away from their native lands, originate as stowaways in the holds of cargo ships. This is not beyond the realm of possibility, but it would not account for most of the Monarchs seen in southwestern England. If such a large, spectacular butterfly left a ship docked at Liverpool or at a port farther north such as Glasgow, it would not go unnoticed in that densely populated area, noted for its abundance of gardeners and nature lovers. There is, of course, little doubt that alien wildlife *can* enter a country in this manner. Some naturalists believe that a few of the Mourning Cloak or Camberwell Beauty butterflies seen in Britain arrive as hibernating butterflies in loads of wood from Scandinavia. I have seen both tarantula and black widow spiders cause a certain amount of consternation in dockside warehouses by scurrying out from among the crates of imported fruit!

## Sleeping Locations, Sleeping Assemblies and Hibernation Sites

Years ago, when my son was quite young, I came across a very simple but rather nice children's book entitled *Where Does the Butterfly Go When It Rains?* This book was intended to encourage a child to observe and to think, yet as I sat reading with my son on my knee, warm and cosy in front of the fire, it set me wondering too. Where indeed do butterflies go when it rains, or when it is too hot, or at night?

There is so much we do not know, even about apparently simple subjects such as this. Most naturalists seem to assume that butterflies just seek shelter when necessary in any convenient hole or cavity, natural or otherwise. But is this correct?

Some individual butterflies do indeed go into holes on occasion, but others stay outside among vegetation when a storm threatens or night comes. Many butterflies crawl down a grass stem into denser vegetation at

*A "sleeping assembly" of European or Essex Skippers, August 7, 1980, at the Memorial University Botanical Garden. In Canada these little Skippers can build up their local populations to pest proportions. They seem to prefer dry, grassy, weedy habitats, and appear quite at home in city waste lots. They can be attracted easily into the home garden if rough grass is present.*

these times. There are advantages and disadvantages in this response. It is warmer and more sheltered nearer the ground, but the butterfly is closer to a multitude of enemies such as spiders, carnivorous beetles, shrews and toads. I have seen the Silver Bordered Fritillary, the Clouded Sulphur, the Dorcas Copper, the Red Admiral, the European or Essex Skipper and the British Ringlet behave in this manner.

If a butterfly settles in the grass for an extended period – for instance, at night to sleep – it will more than likely position itself head down and fold its wings tightly over its body. This attitude possibly helps to protect it from a lowering atmospheric temperature, and also renders it less visible to potential enemies on account of the cryptic appearance of its underwings. Many butterflies, the Mourning Cloak for instance, turn in for the night remarkably early, at about six o'clock, no matter how warm and bright the weather, yet the Red Admiral will often hang on until the last minute of sunshine, seemingly trying to extract the maximum possible benefit from every ray. But no butterfly, to the best of my knowledge, is ever active in the gloaming, as is the large *Aeshna* dragonfly, for instance.

Most butterflies sleep by themselves, but there are species that under certain circumstances congregate to sleep together in considerable numbers. The Monarch is one of the well-known species that does this. In their migration south they can sometimes be observed sleeping together in hundreds and possibly thousands, on suitable bushes or trees. Some *Heliconiidae* butterflies such as the Zebra are reputed to gather together into sleeping colonies at night and to disperse for feeding during the day. Certain Swallowtails and the Small Blue, the Chalk Hill Blue, and possibly the Brown Argus of Britain are also thought to form sleeping assemblies, but I have never come across one. My only experience of sleeping assemblies has been with the European or Essex Skipper. Whenever I have seen an assembly, the numbers have been rather small, a dozen or so individuals. Only once have I seen a substantial number together. On that occasion I counted over a hundred butterflies in an area of rough grass of approximately 1 square metre (3 square feet). Some seed heads of timothy grass were adorned with three and four Skippers. It was a warm evening in early August, and it was rapidly getting dark when I discovered them, so I could not risk making a really accurate count in case I disturbed the creatures, but by using a flash unit I was able to take some splendid coloured photographs. Interestingly enough, every one of these Skippers was sleeping head up; not one was head down, in the reputed manner of many species. Whether or not this sleeping position is a particular characteristic of Skippers I can't say.

Butterflies often shelter beneath a large leaf or among dense vegetation during heavy rain. I once found a Mourning Cloak sheltering beneath a bushy piece of groundsel, a weed common in both England and Newfoundland, and I have often seen Red Admirals fly up and settle underneath the dense, relatively waterproof branches of conifers, especially those covered in lichens, at the start of inclement weather or as evening approaches. But there are always exceptions to the rule. I once photographed an Inornate Ringlet, a butterfly very similar to the Small Heath of Britain, clinging fully exposed to a stalk of heather during a prolonged spell of cold drizzle. It was as attractive as a sculpture of beautiful, tiny, translucent water globules.

Both Milbert's Tortoise Shells and Mourning Cloaks have been observed in the Botanical Garden entering woodpiles in early evening. These observations, in fact, were what caused me to scatter additional, specially constructed log piles in appropriate sites around the less developed parts of the garden.

In Britain, a land of gardeners, it is said that butterflies will regularly enter garden sheds for shelter. When I was a boy in Britain, long before the advent of central heating, we often found small Tortoise Shell and Peacock butterflies wintering behind the wardrobe or among the folds of heavy curtains. In the Botanical Garden the greenhouse door is often left wide open late into the evening during the summer. The open door seems to tempt lone individuals of several species deliberately to take temporary shelter inside. I have found the Red Admiral, the Small White, the Painted Lady, the Green Comma, the Essex Skipper and the White Admiral there from time to time. This deliberate behaviour is different from that of butterflies that blunder into such death traps by chance during the heat of a midsummer's day.

Though butterflies are sun lovers, they do not normally venture abroad in extremely hot, bright weather. In Newfoundland, when we happen to have an occasional prolonged hot spell with temperatures up to 27°C (80°F), our butterflies take a midday siesta, during which they are likely to hide away in the shade somewhere. I have photographed a Tiger Swallowtail hanging, wings closed, just out of the sun among a shaded mixture of grass and wild raspberry canes, and have seen other butterflies in similar situations.

The sleeping shelters and locations that butterflies seek out to escape from heat or rain are, I think, used as temporary retreats. Butterflies that overwinter must find more permanent shelter if they are to survive.

For a permanent site to be suitable for overwintering butterflies, it must be able to provide shelter from such perils as driving rain or sleet, desiccating winds, erratically fluctuating temperatures and direct winter sunlight, and also, if possible, protection from predators such as birds and shrews. Only a few species of butterfly can withstand extreme cold, but a dry, constant cold does not always seem to be the major cause of butterfly deaths during the winter months. If it were, how could the Mourning Cloak withstand the Arctic blast of a Canadian winter and yet be unable to survive the relatively mild winter of the British Isles? I believe the answer to the question of butterfly survival during the winter has more to do with high

*Overleaf:*
*When I was a boy in Britain, before central heating was popular, it was a common experience to find butterflies overwintering in suburban homes. Butterflies entered through open windows in the late summer or early autumn, seeking out cool nooks and crannies in which to hibernate, away from the wet, the drafts and the winter sunlight. We usually had a few Small Tortoise Shells and Peacocks tucked in behind the wardrobe, the chest of drawers, or the ancient curtains. When the spring sun warmed the rooms again, these butterflies would become restless, so we would fling the windows wide open lest they beat themselves to death against the panes. Here, two of these fragile creatures have tucked themselves against the picture and beneath the bookcase to sit out the long, dreary weeks of winter.*

EDWARD

BATH

humidity than with extreme cold. The lengthy periods of muggy weather during the British winter encourage the growth of mildews, which are extremely detrimental to hibernating butterflies. There are other reasons why butterflies should avoid excessive dampness, one being that dry tissues can be supercooled even without killing ice being formed. Scientists also believe that the body fluid of a butterfly contains a type of antifreeze that prevents it from freezing solid.

Where do overwintering butterflies establish themselves to while away their hibernation? There is no doubt that many like to crawl into some dark, dry place such as a deep fissure in a rock face or a cavity in a dry-stone wall or log pile. They may also crawl in among dead leaves that are caught in some dry, sheltered place. They certainly will hide away inside hollow trees or tuck themselves behind the exfoliating bark of rotting tree trunks. They will also stow away in sheds, attics and the awkward corners of overhanging eaves.

One of the few things that can be said in favour of our modern rubbish dumps and the derelict cars strewn around our Newfoundland countryside, is that they furnish overwintering sites for some of our butterflies. One well-known American butterfly expert once found six species of Brushfooted butterfly or *Nymphalidae* in a rubbish dump on a single February afternoon. I have never seen this sort of thing myself; I loathe winter with a passion and have never managed to bring myself to look for butterflies in this unprepossessing season.

Some types of evergreen vegetation, if growing in a suitable situation, can provide a warm, snug shelter for overwintering butterflies. For instance, in Britain the Brimstone butterfly will often tuck itself away among the ivy (*Hedera helix*) that grows profusely on the walls of so many old houses and up the trunks of the ancient trees that are so numerous in the rural areas of that country. Overwintering butterflies must also find sanctuary in the large clumps or expanses of rhododendrons established on the grounds of ancient estates, just as foxes find dry, concealed refuge on the ground beneath them, and many birds a roosting place under the leathery umbrella of their broad, ever-green leaves. It is surprising how little moisture and wind penetrate to the centre of a good-sized rhododendron. The protection they afford is one of the very few justifications for planting these shrubs in a garden established primarily for butterflies.

Of course not all butterflies overwinter in the adult or imago stage. Of all of our butterfly species, the percentage that passes the winter in this stage is rather small. A far greater number go through the winter months as eggs, caterpillars, or chrysalids.

It has always been a wonder to me how insects, particularly butterflies, manage to survive winter in any stage of their development. When you think how deep the frost can penetrate into the ground and how easily we humans get frostbite, it seems remarkable that the tiny egg or caterpillar of a butterfly can come through it all and continue its normal development once the spring rolls around again. Take the North American Bog Copper, for instance. This tiny butterfly lays its eggs on one of the native cranberries that inhabit sphagnum bogs. These prostrate plants, together with any eggs adhering to them, spend the winter frozen to the bog's surface, sometimes under or within a layer of ice. Even though there is often a blanket of snow to protect them from desiccation by wind, they have adapted to survival in a very hostile climate indeed. Britain, of course, does not usually have low winter temperatures like much of North America's, but it does have prolonged and nasty cold snaps. Under normal winter conditions the eggs of the tiny Purple Hairstreak and the Essex Skipper come through unharmed, though the latter does tuck its eggs into a coiled-up blade of grass that may offer some slight protection. Actually, such a spot is probably more useful as a protection against hungry birds than as an insulation against frosts. There is some evidence to suggest that eggs can withstand freak weather conditions better than caterpillars can. A fine example occurred in 1953, when the east coast of Essex and Kent in England suffered particularly bad winter floods. Caterpillars died in great numbers, but the eggs of the Essex Skipper came through in grand style. Their survival could, of course, simply reflect the fact that eggs have a lower metabolic rate and therefore need less oxygen.

I find it difficult to think of an egg as a living, breathing creature, but with a tiny caterpillar it is easy. One may well wonder how this tiny morsel of living tissue can live through a winter, especially a Canadian winter, without having all of its body cells frozen and blasted apart by temperatures that can quickly kill a fully-clothed human or cause the sea to freeze over. Yet despite the elements many species of butterfly do overwinter here as caterpillars. In my own locality, for instance, the Pink Edged Sulphur, the Pearl Crescent and the Arctic Skipper pass the winter as older caterpillars. In Britain caterpillars of two particularly beautiful species, the Purple Emperor and the Marbled White, overwinter. On both sides of the Atlantic some Fritillary caterpillars go into hibernation as soon as they emerge from the egg. They eat the egg shell, and then tuck themselves away to await the spring, when they must quickly sally forth to find food before starvation hits.

Some overwintering caterpillars construct a winter shelter for themselves. This shelter is known as a "hibernaculum." The best example on both sides of the Atlantic is the caterpillar of the White Admiral butterfly. When partly grown this caterpillar cuts away the forward part of a leaf, usually about half, and then folds the two sides of the remainder up over its midrib, sealing them together with silk. In this way it forms a leaf tube. It then seals off the end nearest the branch, and makes the leaf more secure by reinforcing the stalk where it joins the twig with numerous strands of silk. Once the

*The Brimstone of Britain overwinters as an adult, tucked away among dense ivy or other suitable cover. During unseasonably warm spells it may appear on the wing remarkably early in the year. Its rich butter-yellow colouring is believed by some authorities to be the source of the term "butterfly."*

hibernaculum is ready, the caterpillar will not wander far from it, but will continue feeding on nearby leaves until ready to hide away inside it for the winter. In Newfoundland hibernation commences towards the end of August and lasts until around June 12.

Many butterflies hibernate in the chrysalis stage. The Swallowtails and the Whites are good examples. In preparation, the caterpillar must seek out a suitably secluded and sheltered resting place, where it can undergo the change and where its new stage, the chrysalis, can remain unharmed until the following spring. There are also caterpillars that just fall to the ground, and pupate inside a dead, curled-up leaf or beneath accumulating leaf litter. In Newfoundland the Spring Azure and the Silvery Blue do this. A few butterfly species have the ability to overwinter as either caterpillar or chrysalis. The Speckled Wood, a quietly handsome butterfly of the British woodlands and hedgerows, is said to be unique among that country's butterflies because it has this ability. Not all butterflies hibernate or pause significantly in their development. For some there is no need, for they do not live in a geographical area of noticeable seasonal change. In Canada and Britain, however, all species must have some way to overwinter safely; if not, they must either migrate or die.

Regardless of how or in what stage a butterfly passes the winter, or indeed any period of its life, its survival is by no means assured. Its existence is being continually threatened by external forces, some of which I shall be discussing briefly later in this chapter.

**Aggression, Territorialism and Relationship with Other Creatures** Most readers will have heard at one time or another that the two strongest instincts in animals are self-preservation and procreation. These two urges are at the root of all animal behaviour and are particularly obvious in aggression and territorialism. Most of us find it easy enough to imagine leopards or grizzly bears being aggressive and defending territories, but we are surprised to hear that, relative to their size, butterflies can be equally belligerent. They appear to be such gentle, fragile creatures that we can hardly visualize them throwing their weight around. But they do.

The Monarch, for instance, has a special aversion for the ruby-throated hummingbird of eastern North America. Since they are both nectar feeders and are similar in size, this dislike is understandable. More surprising is the fact that the Pearl Crescent, a small Brushfooted butterfly of North America with a wing span of less than 4 centimetres (1.5 inches), has been known to attack not only birds, but also dogs and people! I have never been threatened by a butterfly myself, I must add.

Aggressive behaviour in butterflies is more often observed between two butterflies or between a butterfly and some other type of insect. With Painted Lady butterflies it is quite common. They have a tendency to attack and drive away from their chosen airspace anything small enough to be taken seriously. In the Botanical Garden they will regularly attack similar-sized butterflies such as the Red Admiral, the Milbert's Tortoise Shell and the Mourning Cloak. Surprisingly, they will sometimes dart up from the flower beds and vigorously harass one of the *Aeshna* dragonflies that patrol the area. Since this large dragonfly in its normal role is a predator of butterflies, I wonder why it does not just turn right about and demolish the nuisance. Maybe like the bald eagle or kestrel falcon chased by a small bird, it just cannot be bothered. I have also seen the Green Comma butterfly rise and attack these dragonflies, and the Jutta Arctic explode off a sphagnum bog to drive a common skimmer dragonfly (*Libellula quadrimaculata*) off its territory. The Grayling butterflies of Britain have the reputation of pursuing not only dragonflies, but also other butterflies and sometimes birds as well.

I have not as yet seen a Mourning Cloak use aerial aggression towards a butterfly or other insect, though I did once see one walk across a flat-topped flower cluster of lance-leaved goldenrod, bodily bump off a Red Admiral established there, and then start to feed at exactly the same site. I am not suggesting that butterflies can think or reason, but the action did seem very deliberate and purposeful.

Some butterflies will position themselves on a convenient perch from which they dash out to investigate other butterflies or to harass other insects. This is their way of checking for a suitable mate while keeping their territory clear of rival males and other unwelcome visitors. White Admirals will use a site well up in a tree, whereas the British Speckled Wood, a small butterfly, prefers lower down so that it can defend a patch of sunlight warming the woodland floor. As the sun moves across the sky and the patch of sunlight crosses its territory, this attractive little butterfly will follow, maintaining its claim to its place in the sun.

The British Small Copper and certain Skippers are among those butterflies that live close to the ground and prefer to use the top of a weed or seed head of grass from which to make their sortie. Some years ago during a beautiful warm but windy afternoon in mid-June, I settled down in a patch of rough grass at my back door to watch an Arctic or Checkered Skipper I had just located there. The grass is on a bankside surrounded by conifer trees, and on this occasion it was quite sheltered. The butterfly was apparently a male, and was busily laying claim to an area of grass and wildflowers of approximately 37 square metres (400 square feet). During the two hours I watched it, it made five attacks on individual McIsaac's Ringlets, one attack on a pair of these butterflies, and one threatening flight towards a bumblebee that droned across its territory like a Lancaster bomber heading home. After a disturbance, this little butterfly would invariably return to perch in the same clump of grass, but it moved from the favoured site as the afternoon drew on and the sun crossed the sky. It made sure it stayed in the sun. Twice I was able to encourage it to land on my hand by slowly bringing my finger from below and having it step onto it. Then, though the weather was good and I looked for it again over the next few days, it disappeared. However, six days later at the same site I came across a rather worn male coupled to a much fresher and somewhat larger female, so its efforts seemed to have paid off. I was delighted at this encounter because these Skippers, though possibly widely distributed in Newfoundland, are certainly not common. In the Botanical Garden we probably have fewer than a dozen small sites that are suitable for them, while seven individuals at three different sites is the greatest number I have seen during any single day.

Butterflies can sometimes be fooled into attacking inanimate objects. I discovered this purely by accident while on a camping trip with a friend deep in the Labrador wilderness. It was a beautiful day, and we were spending it hunting for alpine plants on a steep and rugged mountainside. Around midday we settled down for a bit of a rest and a bite to eat. It was a quiet, restful spot, with a pair of rough-legged hawks sailing in the blue sky above, and a lone stag caribou swimming across a lake about 600 metres (2 000 feet) below. Absent-mindedly I tossed a small stone down the mountainside to the left of us, and was startled to see a medium-sized butterfly leap up and give chase. The creature was perched on a sun-warmed boulder and apparently resented anything that moved in its general area. Naturally we flicked a few more small stones into its area to see what would happen. Each time a stone went bouncing past, the butterfly shot out and gave chase for a considerable stretch down the mountainside. We could not get a satisfactory look at this butterfly, but from its general appearance we believed it to be either a White Veined Arctic or a Polixenes Arctic, both known to occur in the general area.

Not all butterflies are aggressive, and even those inclined to be antisocial are not so all the time. Many butterflies, including the Painted Lady, congregate peacefully while nectaring from flowers, especially in the fall. It is sometimes possible to see Mourning Cloaks, Milbert's Tortoise Shells, Red Admirals, Painted Ladies, Compton Tortoise Shells, Small Whites, Green Commas and the occasional American Painted Lady fluttering about and feeding with one another in some warm corner of a flowery meadow.

The aggression characteristic of some butterflies does not, as far as I know, adversely affect the efforts of the butterfly gardener. A particularly pugnacious individual might keep some butterflies out of a very small garden, but I doubt it would make much difference to the density of butterflies in a larger one. Also, the flight periods of the various species are relatively short, so the population of local butterflies will be regularly changing.

In nature, any occurrence, no matter how small, will have an influence of some kind on other components of the living system. Many ecologists call this principle "the web of life" – a term that suggests how activity of any sort in even the smallest part of the system will cause movement or reaction elsewhere and possibly throughout the whole. It is easy to see that the actions of certain other species of wildlife will affect butterflies. Their enemies are an obvious subject for consideration, and I will discuss these shortly. But there are other things in nature that affect the lives of butterflies in a less obvious way.

*Arctic or Checkered Skippers on bog laurel (*Kalmia polifolia*), St. John's Narrows, Newfoundland, June 19, 1983. On a bright day with the wind off the land, this fascinating and rather scarce little butterfly has left the grass on a patch of damp ground to hunt for nectar on the adjacent shore. Though this butterfly does visit my garden occasionally, I have found very few plants that will hold it there. A sight such as the one depicted here is a rarity to be treasured.*

Take, for instance, the grazing or browsing of cattle, sheep, rabbits, hares and game such as deer and moose. I briefly discussed the grazing of grasslands in the chapter on habitats, and will only add here that the depressions made by the hooves of cows and horses are known to provide sites in which Blues and other small butterflies may sun and gain shelter from the wind. It is sometimes surprising how much warmer than that of the surrounding area the ground air can be in a slight depression exposed to the sun.

In my own part of Canada browsers rather than grazers likely have an influence on butterflies. Moose and snowshoe hares will often feed on the end shoots of branches of deciduous shrubs and small trees. As a result, the branches tend to bush out, and so provide more foliage and thus more forage for the caterpillars of butterflies such as the Tiger Swallowtail, the Mourning Cloak and the White Admiral. Such browsing will at times also stimulate certain shrubs to produce more flowers, and these in turn will provide more nectar and, in the case of withrod and other viburnums, more flowers and seeds for the caterpillars of the Spring Azure butterfly to feed upon.

Any mammal such as the rabbit, prairie dog, badger, fox, or mole that brings up fresh earth to the surface, may create suitable environments for the germination and growth of grasses and wildflowers of benefit to butterflies. Where the surface is disturbed by the pawing or fighting of stag deer or caribou, or by the huge bull moose, butterflies may be similarly benefited.

The industrious beaver is famous for its ability to change the environment. When these animals inhabit an area, their influence on other wildlife is substantial. They affect butterflies in a number of minor ways. In felling the trees they feed upon, they open up the forest, letting in the sunlight and so encouraging the growth of a more varied and often more beneficial flora. Their need for additional stretches of water causes them to flood the land around their lodges and so kill the adjacent conifer trees. The trees eventually rot and provide foraging and nesting sites for woodpeckers. Abandoned woodpecker nesting holes may provide shelter and overwintering sites for butterflies. The freshly-cut stumps of deciduous trees bleed sap, especially in the spring, and around here the sap provides food for the Compton Tortoise Shell, the Mourning Cloak, the Green Comma, the Red Admiral and the Milbert's Tortoise Shell. Sap is also made temporarily available by the activities of insects such as the willow borer and birds such as the yellow-bellied sapsucker. Even when our native bears stretch up and claw the trees, the resulting sap flow is probably made use of by butterflies. In Britain the Red Admiral, the Comma, the Peacock, the Holly Blue and the rare Large Tortoise Shell are known to feed from sap; the Large Tortoise Shell is even said to prefer it to nectar.

Many of the interactions between butterflies and other animals are of little significance to the average butterfly gardener. Yet these interactions go on in the natural world daily, and many of them could probably be turned to practical account in our butterfly gardening efforts.

**The Enemies of Butterflies** It seems a shame that creatures as beautiful as butterflies should have enemies in the form of predators, parasites, diseases and so on. But as with all living things, if they are to maintain healthy, viable populations, there must be some form of population control. Still, there are times, particularly in a less than perfect summer, when I wish the natural controls were not so effective.

What are these controls, and how do butterflies react to them? One of the greatest problems facing butterflies both in North America and in Britain is unseasonable weather, particularly warm, damp winters and severe, late frosts. There is really nothing the butterfly gardener can do about this sort of thing. The enthusiast can only put up with it and mutter under his breath, meanwhile hoping the damage will not be too great.

Warm, damp winters are particularly bad for causing moulds and fungus damage to overwintering butterflies in the chrysalis or imago stage. Also, disease caused by viruses and bacteria can decimate butterfly populations even in good summer weather, particularly if caterpillars are present in high densities. Dead or dying caterpillars can be found at such times limply hanging among vegetation or lying in pools of fluid on the leaves of their host plants. Very little is known about these butterfly diseases.

But unpleasant weather may not always be detrimental to local butterflies. In Britain, for instance, it is now believed that the colder Aprils experienced over the past couple of decades have caused an increase in the Orange Tip butterfly population by encouraging them to stay in the overwintering chrysalis stage until later in the spring. Since plants will start into life and continue to grow at cooler temperatures than the average butterfly will venture forth to feed in, a cooler spring will in certain circumstances ensure that more plants are advanced enough to be in flower when the temperature rises sufficiently to bring out the butterflies.

In nature, most species are hosts to parasites. Butterflies are no exception; several parasitic flies and wasps prey on their eggs, caterpillars and chrysalids. Many adult butterflies have red mites or other tiny creatures as parasites. The Marbled White of Britain appears to be particularly susceptible to such pests.

I never cease to wonder at the ways of nature, and am forever being surprised by what I see. One summer I collected a couple of Tiger Swallowtail eggs from off a mountain ash bush in the garden, and placed them in a closed container to await emergence from them. Some days later I noticed that one egg had gone particularly dark and so suspected it had a parasite. Interested in seeing what type of beast came out, I placed the egg in a tiny glass vial and sealed it tight. Next day a hole appeared in the egg wall, and I carefully scrutinized inside the vial with a 10 X magnifying glass. A Swallowtail's egg is about the size of a pin-head, so I knew that whatever had emerged must be very small and difficult to see. Imagine my surprise when I counted not one, but thirteen fully-grown, perfectly-formed parasitic wasps flitting around, dodging each other and alighting on the glass to stroke their antennae. They were later identified as *Trichogramma retorridum*. I have since had the same thing happen with a Pink Edged Sulphur's egg, but this time only five wasps appeared.

Caterpillars are of course particularly susceptible to parasitic wasps and flies. Though the parasite's egg is laid on or through the skin of the caterpillar, it is often not until the chrysalis stage is reached that the wasp emerges. Caterpillars gathered from the wild and hand-reared are often found to be spoiled in this way. I once had three different types of wasps emerge from some Spring Azure or Holly Blue caterpillars collected in the wild. They spent the winter inside the chrysalis and emerged the following spring.

In my area there is also a fly, possibly a tachinid fly, that looks something like a small bluebottle fly and that is a caterpillar parasite. The fly must lay its egg on the caterpillar where its maggot, when emerged, can burrow through the skin and into the body. Only one maggot is present in each caterpillar, but they grow to about 1 centimetre (0.39 inch) in length and half that in width. They look very much like the maggots or "gentles" that British coarse fishermen use as bait for roach, perch and so on. Though the whole thought is rather unpleasant, I find it remarkable that this parasite can live, grow and actually move about inside the caterpillar without damaging anything vital. The internal structure of a caterpillar is quite simple, but even so, the parasite must have a very good instinct for knowing just what it can and cannot consume. When the caterpillar should be preparing to pupate, it becomes lethargic, and instead of pupation taking place the maggot pops out through the skin and the caterpillar dies.

Parasites probably destroy quite a large segment of the butterfly population at different stages of the life cycle. I have seen fifty percent of a brood of Mourning Cloak caterpillars destroyed by the parasitic fly I have just described. It has been suggested that attack from ichneumon wasps decimates as much as ninety-nine percent of the Large Tortoise Shell population in Britain yearly – a terrible situation, if true.

A caterpillar is unable to do much to protect itself against such dangers. The Monarch caterpillar is said to be able to wipe off parasitic wasps with one of its two pairs of long, soft, blackish filaments, but whether this is true, or whether the action is particularly effective, is uncertain. Some caterpillars automatically drop off their food plant to the ground if they are disturbed, and others stay hidden, coming out to feed only in the dark. Both these characteristics of behaviour must be of some protective advantage.

One of the worst predators of butterflies in my experience, certainly in the botanical garden and nature reserve under my care, is the spider. Spiders not only ensnare many adult butterflies in their webs, but also cause the death of a considerable number of caterpillars. Here we seem to have a very high population of one of the common species of garden spiders, commonly called the cross spider. It is fairly large, has a cross on its back, and produces particularly strong, sticky silk that is capable of holding fast large butterflies, grasshoppers and the strong *Aeshna* dragonflies. I am forever getting this silk across my face or stuck to my hands when I work in the garden. I can well understand why some North American birds such as the hummingbird and the blue-gray gnatcatcher, as well as the British long-tailed titmouse, use this material in their nest building, and how these silken webs will hold small, relatively weak butterflies such as the Bog Copper. In the Botanical Garden, however, I am more likely to see the larger species such as the Tiger Swallowtail, the Red Admiral, the Mourning Cloak and the White Admiral in these webs.

Whenever I see a butterfly hit a spider's web, or whenever I come across one that has only recently become ensnared, I suffer through the dilemma of whether or not to free it. It is often difficult to remove spider silk from a butterfly without damaging the creature, and there remains the question of whether we should or shouldn't. Spiders too have to live. Strictly speaking, I expect we should let nature take its course in the natural countryside, but in the human-created butterfly garden I am no longer sure. Spiders too have enemies, and uninhabited webs or sticky supporting strands can entrap when there is no spider in residence to use the entrapped food. Anyway, rightly or wrongly I carry a walking stick and use it to reach into flower beds to knock down webs and silken stringers. It is particularly important to destroy webs situated in openings between two taller clumps of flowers where butterflies may well pass.

Not all types of spider build webs to capture their food; some just lie in wait and pounce on unsuspecting prey, and others go forth deliberately to stalk their food. The so-called "flower spiders" are very well camouflaged, and lie in wait on or very close to a flower head; other species forage among the stems and leaves of plants, seeking out something to overpower and consume. These latter ones destroy a large number of caterpillars in our garden, particularly the earlier stages of our Short Tailed Swallowtail caterpillars. As far as I know, there is nothing the butterfly gardener can do about foraging spiders, short of caging all the valuable resident caterpillars – which is neither necessary nor possible.

As I have said, dragonflies are responsible for a fair share of butterfly deaths. Unfortunately, these beautifiul insects are also in need of a helping hand to ensure their continued presence in some parts of the world's over-manipulated countryside. Dragonflies require wet habitats. Sadly, these habitats are being destroyed in many areas of North America and Britain by drainage schemes, landfill projects and the seepage of toxic chemical residue from adjacent farmlands.

A well-landscaped pond adds beauty to any garden, and if some of its water is made to dampen the surrounding soil, it will provide a suitable site for butterfly host plants such as violets and lady's smock and for nectar sources such as joe-pye weed. However, a pond can also provide a breeding site for a variety of dragonflies. If you want to protect your butterflies, you should put a few fish in the pond to eat the dragonfly larvae, but if you are more concerned with creating a natural, well-balanced area where all wildlife is equally important, then you must allow the dragonflies to breed, and not begrudge them the butterflies they take.

Incidentally, dragonflies often have to work hard for the insects they capture. Butterflies can at times maneuvre remarkably well, and will zig-zag admirably in their attempt to shake off a pursuing dragonfly. They will also retreat into vegetable cover, and even suddenly close their wings in midflight, dropping to earth as if made of stone. Though I have not observed this particular strategy very often, I can well recall seeing both Painted Ladies and Pink Edged Sulphurs use it to advantage. Once, a newly-emerged Painted Lady was fluttering around some blooms in our display of old-fashioned flowers, when a cruising *Aeshna* dragonfly spotted it and zeroed in. The butterfly took defensive action by zig-zagging through the air for about 3 metres (10 feet) and then dropping vertically to earth. Here it stayed for just over a minute, and then fluttered up onto an *Iberis* "hyacinth" flower and started to sun itself. When another *Aeshna*, or the same one again, came cruising by shortly afterwards, the butterfly immediately flicked its wings tightly shut, and remained in this position until well after the danger had gone.

In Newfoundland cruising dragonflies of several different species are plentiful. They appear to feed mainly on the smaller insects, and no doubt make life out of doors more bearable for us by consuming untold numbers of our noxious mosquitoes and black flies. In the Botanical Garden, which is about 45 hectares (110 acres), we have found space to dig a few shallow ponds to encourage these insects. We seem particularly to have benefited a small, white-faced *Sympetrum* dragonfly that does not, as far as I know, tackle anything as large as a butterfly.

Many of us find it difficult to reconcile ourselves to a nature "red in tooth and claw." In the small garden or suburban reserve maintained primarily for the welfare of butterflies, it is clearly better not to create or maintain habitats that are of particular benefit to their predators. Even so, tolerating birds and dragonflies in a butterfly garden meant to be enjoyed by humans may prove to be the lesser of two evils. In Newfoundland, for instance, and in many areas of North America, enjoyment of the countryside can be significantly lessened for many people because of the presence of biting flies, which are often found in great abundance. When an outdoor facility is maintained from the public purse, the pressure on its administrative staff to resort to chemical sprays for controlling biting insects can be significant. Since very few sprays, if any, are specific to one family of insects, the potential danger to butterflies is great, so whenever possible it is better to avoid insecticides altogether and to try to control pest insects by other, more natural, means. One method, the one I ascribe to, is to maintain a more diverse and ecologically integrated environment. If such an environment is supported by thoughtful management practices – for instance, by the judicious thinning of trees and scrub to allow wind to blow away biting flies – and by the acceptance of all naturally occurring wildlife, including dragonflies and birds, then I think the local butterfly populations are better off in the long run. Even in the small-scale home garden, the gardener who wants to keep flowers, shrubs and trees in an acceptable condition without the use of toxic chemicals, must strive to create and maintain plant and animal diversity. The term "acceptable" is, of course, relative. If perfect blooms in clinically pleasing surroundings are your reason for being, you might as well not try to become a butterfly gardener or the owner of a mini–nature reserve! Of course none of this is quite as clear-cut as it sounds, and we who are fortunate enough to start our butterfly gardens on a piece of near-natural habitat are better off than those faced with the desolation of churned-up subsoil and builders' refuse that so often accompanies a newly-constructed home.

Anyway, whether we like it or not, birds are efficient predators of butterflies, particularly at the caterpillar stage. Warblers especially are always on the look-out to find and consume caterpillars, and many other birds, even the humble house sparrow, include caterpillars in their diets as an easily digested source of protein for their nestlings.

Other birds such as swallows, martins and flycatchers also take their toll. They are adept at seizing butterflies on the wing. Not every attack finishes with a meal, however. Many a butterfly escapes simply because the bird aims to grab hold of it by the wing, which is a fragile thing, prone to tearing. The captured butterfly, vigorously wriggling about, often causes its wings to tear, and so makes its escape but leaves behind a somewhat bemused bird with a triangular piece of useless material in its beak. If you have ever taken more than just a casual interest, you are probably already familiar with the V-shaped cuts at the outer edges of butterflies' wings.

The wing markings of some butterflies are said to have evolved as targets to attract a bird's attention away from the more vulnerable head and body. These markings are sometimes referred to as "deflection spots."

When at rest with their wings tightly closed, many butterflies are protected by being remarkably well-camouflaged by their dull or cryptic colouration. Other butterflies deliberately orient themselves to the sun when they are resting on the ground. They alight, close their wings, and then carefully tilt themselves at an extremely acute angle so that the flattened undersurface of one wing faces upwards towards the sun. Very little shadow is cast on the ground to give away their location, and still the maximum amount of warmth is absorbed. The Grayling of Britain is famous for this behaviour, and here the tiny Brown Elfin is just as adept at the technique.

The Monarch, both caterpillar and adult, has a very unpleasant taste that birds soon learn to avoid. The Viceroy butterfly, though very similar in appearance to the Monarch, is not distasteful, but as a "mimic" it gains protection when associating with Monarchs. The Monarchs must of course far outnumber the Viceroys, or the deception would soon be noticed.

Many butterflies have wings that are brightly coloured on their upper side but dull underneath. The colourful upper surface is used for display, and the cryptic undersurface provides concealment. Butterflies usually keep their wings closed for concealment, except when absorbing heat from the sun. If disturbed by a bird or other creature while resting with their wings closed, some butterflies will speedily flick open their wings to flash their bright colours. This action sometimes so startles the potential aggressor that it withdraws. The Peacock butterfly of Britain, which has a very colourful and noticeable eyespot on the upper surface of each wing, frequently uses this technique. And I have seen Red Admirals use it to good advantage on several occasions in the Botanical Garden.

Butterflies have other enemies too. Toads and frogs are always mentioned, but my belief is that they prey on moths more than on butterflies. Other insects take a toll. Certain bugs will suck butterfly eggs whenever they find them, and some beetles and wasps are reputed to be deadly for caterpillars, and even eat adult butterflies if they happen to catch them off guard at rest or asleep. Some say that wasps and robber flies will even attack and destroy adults in flight. The ever-hungry shrew needs to consume anything and everything it can overpower if it is to maintain its tremendous metabolic rate, so it will take any caterpillar, chrysalis, or adult it chances upon.

Newfoundland has no indigenous shrews, but twenty-odd years ago the forestry service introduced some to combat the larch sawfly. The offspring of the tiny mammals spread over the island quite rapidly and turned up in the Botanical Garden shortly after I started it. I believe that the populations of a number of species of Hawkmoth have diminished as a result, but I have no supporting scientific data. Their large, succulent caterpillars are well within the reach of shrews when they descend to the earth to hunt up a place to pupate, and the large pupae are usually situated not too deep among the leaf litter and are easy prey.

The ever-popular house cat can develop a real knack for batting butterflies out of the air. This is sport, of course, not a need for food. Cats are great wanderers, and they destroy more small wildlife than some people may imagine. Batting butterflies out of the air for sport used to be a popular summer pastime for some children too. It appears to be far less common nowadays, but it is still indulged in now and again, like the "sport" of swiping bats out of the air with a tennis racket! Human beings in general have the most profound effect, either detrimental or beneficial, on butterfly populations – but that is the subject of a later chapter.

It can be a source of wonder, how any butterflies at all are able to get through the life cycle to breed and perpetuate their kind. Actually, under normal circumstances there need be no worry about a species' continued existence because, among other things, butterflies have evolved a capacity to lay more eggs than are required. Indeed, if all the eggs that are laid made it to the adult stage, the result would be a disaster both for butterflies and for us.

**Mud Puddling and Such** For some reason not yet fully understood, some kinds of butterflies have a strong inclination to imbibe moisture from damp mud, rotting vegetation, animal excreta and urine, carrion and human perspiration. This activity appears to indicate a need not for water itself, but for a solution from which certain minerals or sodium ions can be extracted.

Butterflies do, of course, require water from time to time, but they will readily suck this up from dew and raindrops. Ample clean supplies are often within easy flying distance of butterflies working the sometimes unpleasant substances I have listed. It has been observed, furthermore, that butterflies drinking from substances with a high moisture content such as mud, do so

*The survival of a healthy fauna depends on many things. Suitable habitats, favourable climatic conditions, freedom from parasites and diseases, and protection from potential predators all play a part in ensuring the continued presence of butterflies and other wild creatures. Predators of butterflies or their caterpillars include birds, dragonflies, spiders, ground beetles, shrews, and sometimes even the family cat. Some pet cats develop a real knack for catching butterflies, but their depredations, though serious in an urban butterfly garden, probably have little adverse effect on butterfly populations in general. The real danger to butterflies is human beings' reckless destruction of natural countryside.*

often without pause and while excreting a drop of clear fluid every ten or so seconds. My wife recently witnessed this phenomenon most clearly. Having just planted and watered-in a couple of rows of beans in her well-manured vegetable garden, she noticed a brilliantly blue male Spring Azure flutter past, plonk itself down on the damp soil, extend its proboscis and commence imbibing moisture. The butterfly was so absorbed in "drinking" that it allowed her to creep up and watch from a distance of about 12 centimetres (5 inches). She then left to fetch me, and I took several photographs of the procedure. I find it remarkable how these creatures can, in such a very short period, extract whatever it is they are extracting and almost immediately excrete the ingested water as a sparkling fluid. This seems to me another clear indication that it is not moisture that is required, but whatever is in it.

There is also, I think, some indication that mud puddling is more common in warmer than in cooler climates. The activity is unusual in this part of Canada, but in the hotter parts of North America it appears to be not at all uncommon during the summer months. But just what is mud puddling? "Mud puddling" is a term used to describe the activity of butterflies that are settled on damp ground or mud and are probing it with their probosces to draw up fluid. Groups of butterflies doing this are referred to as "mud puddle clubs" and are usually made up mostly but not exclusively of male butterflies. These "clubs" are very striking sights when they are made up of many individuals and species; they can be seen in Mexico, Africa and South America. We still have a lot to learn, but many scientists believe that mud puddling indicates a need in the butterfly for amino acids. Males are said to be more active than females and so may require more of this nourishment. When they imbibe amino acids from these sources, the competition for the acids from a nectar base may be greatly lessened and the females allowed more access to the local flowers.

The earth at these sites has usually been enriched by some form of animal or plant waste. There can be a large number of one species of butterfly at the sites, or a mixture of species. The Tiger Swallowtail is possibly the butterfly in North America most famous for mud puddling. A friend of mine once photographed a "club" of approximately 200 of these spectacular butterflies, and they have been recorded in even larger assemblies. One writer tells of seeing 300 gathered at an area downhill from a country cabin that was obviously not blessed with modern plumbing! The largest mud puddle club of these butterflies I have seen was much smaller, just 14 individuals, but it was a thrilling and marvellous sight. I can hardly imagine these large and beautiful butterflies milling around together in a club of several hundred.

Many butterflies seem to enjoy mud puddling. In North America these include the Alfalfa, the Compton Tortoise Shell, the Eastern Tailed Blue, the Buckeye, the Painted Lady, the Pearl Crescent and the Hackberry butterflies. In Newfoundland we have as yet had reports only of the Tiger Swallowtail, the White Admiral and the Pink Edged Sulphur, and of a single Mourning Cloak that I saw probing some damp, recently exposed mineral soil. Once, however, while I was rushing down the hill on one of the nature trails in the Botanical Garden, I believe I flushed five Spring Azures from a tiny damp spot. Unfortunately, I was moving fast and my mind was elsewhere, so I cannot be absolutely sure. In Britain the Wood White, the Common Blue and the White Admiral are mud puddlers.

I have already suggested that mud puddling is associated mainly with hot, dry weather. Certainly the few observations we have had, have all been made in very hot weather. I had an interesting experience in early September of 1981. It was a gloriously sunny, hot day, so I decided to wash the car on the gravel driveway adjacent to my back door. I wasn't giving much thought to butterflies at the time, but suddenly realized I had four Red Admirals probing the fine gravel being wetted by my soapy water. They continued to show interest until I finished washing the car and the gravel dried up.

It appears more than likely that in most instances of this behaviour the butterflies are seeking nothing more than some form of easily absorbed salt, so essential to animal life. Scientists have found they can encourage Tiger Swallowtails to congregate at trays of sand simply by impregnating the sand with a salt solution. There was a rather detailed paper on this very subject in *Science* magazine some years ago. The formula mentioned was well beyond my comprehension, so I asked a chemist friend to sort it all out for me. In case you would like to try attracting butterflies with salt solution, here is an equivalent formula, courtesy of my friend. Make a stock solution by mixing 5 g (1 heaping tsp.) of ordinary table salt into 1 L (1 qt.) of water. When you are ready to use the solution, dilute it by 100 to 1, and use enough of this new solution to soak the sand or mud you have marked for the purpose. You will have to maintain the sand or mud in a damp condition; do so by adding plain water only – the moisture will evaporate, but the salt will not, so you must be careful not to build up the quantity of salt in the area.

Butterflies will sometimes alight on the hand or bare arm of a human during hot, dry weather. This usually happens if the person is or has recently been perspiring, and indicates, of course, that the creature is after the salt we humans excrete in sweat. Many years ago, when I was younger and newer at the game, I was making a small collection for educational purposes of the butterflies to be encountered in Newfoundland's government-run camping and picnic parks. One hot afternoon I was collecting in a park on our west coast and particularly wanted to capture one of the large Tiger Swallowtails that were patrolling the edge of the forest along a new access road. Suddenly rounding a corner, I came across a small group of bare-chested workers frantically waving their shovels around in the air as if a vampire bat had left its home in South America and were threatening to bloat itself with human blood. One sweat-drenched, hefty fellow appeared to be the centre of the melee, which was being caused, believe it or not, by nothing more than a very persistent Tiger Swallowtail doing its best to reach this large, glistening "honeypot" of available salt. After I had managed to quiet the situation down a bit and capture the butterfly, I showed it to them and explained what I thought it had been trying to do. They looked a bit sheepish but took it in good part. It is remarkable, the fear that any kind of insect can inspire in some people.

Here is one more example of salt intake. During the mid-seventies I made a plant-hunting trip to a small limestone gully on a rather out-of-the-way part of our coastline. To reach it I had to take a short small-boat ride across a salt water bay. Though it was a bright, sunny day, there were whitecaps, and the stiffish breeze forced us to use oilskins to stop the flying sea water from soaking us to the skin. Arriving at its destination, a small, sheltered, sunny bay, the boat had hardly reached the shore before two White Admirals alighted on our soaked oilskins and started wandering around, investigating the wet rubber with their probosces. When we took these garments off and laid them in the boat, the butterflies continued to work them until they were dry. Once they were dry, the pair lost interest in them and returned to patrolling the water's edge, probing at the dislodged clumps of seaweed that were not completely out of the water and were still being kept damp by a wick action. White Admirals are not normally associated with the seashore, but in Newfoundland, in the right season, in quiet, sunny coves where the forest almost dips its roots into the sea, they can often be found enjoying the warm microclimates of these sheltered spots.

As I have mentioned, many butterflies seek salt or some other mineral they require by probing such unpleasant substances as animal excreta, urine and decomposing carcasses. These last, of course, are relatively unavailable, so we seldom see butterflies being drawn to them. But I remember one entomologist writing of how he found four different species together imbibing the juices of a dead, decaying bobcat killed on a roadside in California. I have never had such an experience, but on the last day of August in 1981 I came across a Red Admiral on one of the nature trails in the Botanical Garden, probing what at first glance looked like a dog's dropping. On closer examination, it turned out to be a regurgitated mass of undigested and partly digested shrews, possibly from an owl or hawk. I counted five shrews and one bird's foot in this "pellet." The Red Admiral was probing one of the damp, undigested shrews. In Britain the Purple Emperor, the White Admiral and some of the other Nymphalids are well known for their fondness for decaying carcasses. Indeed, in the less enlightened days of rampant butterfly collecting, male Purple Emperors were lured to their death by rotting carcasses staked within reach of a hand net – something, it is to be hoped, this superb creature no longer has to put up with. Decomposition produces sugars that may serve as substitutes for nectar; if they do, here is the reason for the attractiveness of carcasses. As for the other substances, a friend once came across a Pearl Crescent, a Tiger Swallowtail, a Disa Alpine and twenty-two Saepiolus Blues mud puddling in the Thunder Bay area of Ontario on what he had reason to believe was a spot where a black bear had recently urinated.

It certainly appears, then, that butterflies engaged in this activity are trying to obtain some form of salt, mineral, or sugar that they require in

*Tiger Swallowtails mud puddling with Spring Azures. This beautiful and sometimes very common Swallowtail will reputedly congregate by the hundreds at suitable muddy, salt-enriched sites. Though large-scale mud puddling is a familiar sight in many parts of Canada and the United States, it is rarely seen in Newfoundland. Mud puddle clubs are made up mostly of male butterflies.*

greater quantities than they can readily obtain from the normal intake of nectar. As I have said, some scientists believe it is sodium ions they are after, because these ions play an essential role in the butterfly's neuromuscular system. Sodium ions are at low levels in many plants and so are generally not passed on from the caterpillar to the adult. And again, the suggestion is that since male butterflies are more active and so require a greater intake of this salt than do females, they are the ones most often found mud puddling. Finally, gathering together in these "bachelor" clubs may also be a form of social behaviour. Over to the animal behaviourists!

In the less exotic surroundings of the family garden, butterflies will sometimes be seen investigating dog droppings. I have seen Tiger Swallowtails, Red Admirals and Green Commas doing this on my own lawn. Also, I have had Tiger Swallowtails, Spring Azures and White Admirals probing around on the surface of my freshly-manured vegetable garden. The White Admiral of North America is well known for its predilection for animal excreta. Some butterflies will facilitate the extraction of minerals from dried-up droppings by excreting saliva to soften the surface and then absorbing the solution. In Britain the Chalk Hill Blue, the Adonis Blue and the Purple Emperor are well known for probing animal droppings.

Whether the information in these last few paragraphs is of any value to a butterfly gardener is doubtful. Certainly I am not suggesting that you stop cleaning up the dog-doo or litter the ground with other noxious substances! But it does no harm to bear this butterfly behaviour in mind, especially if you happen to be an old-fashioned gardener who still makes up liquid manure in the time-honoured way. Some of this fluid poured on a tray of shallow sand or soil may provide an interesting experiment during a period of particularly warm, dry weather.

Some butterflies enjoy imbibing the juice of rotten fruit. It would not be a bad idea for the enthusiast to attract these insects by providing them with some suitably old fruit. The Red Admiral on both sides of the Atlantic seems to love a fermenting apple, as do the Peacock and the Comma in Britain. The Mourning Cloak here visits fermenting mountain ash, or rowan, berries, and in Europe it is reputed to like the juice of brambles, or blackberries.

I have tried in this chapter to give some small insight into aspects of butterfly habits and behaviour. Some of what I have said, may be of practical value to the butterfly gardener, some may not. But the more we know and understand about butterflies in their natural environment, the better the chance we have of tempting them to visit our own patches of earth.

# Some Thoughts on the Planning, Construction and Planting of the Butterfly Garden

Successful butterfly gardening can be achieved only by the marriage of two enduring loves – the love of gardening and the love of live, free-flying butterflies. There are, of course, butterfly enthusiasts who are not gardeners and gardeners who are not interested in butterflies. But if you are one of the former and yet have now decided to take the plunge and become a butterfly gardener, you will have to learn quickly some of the fundamentals of gardening and the culture of a variety of appropriate plants. Many readers will, I am sure, already have a sound knowledge of gardening, but for those of you who do not, this chapter is written in the hope that it will help you over some of the possible pitfalls. If you think you require more detailed information on any specific aspect of horticulture, check your local library. Also, do not forget to seek the assistance of local experts.

Whether you are starting with an already established garden, a piece of urban wasteland, or a new property devoid of vegetation, your initial approach should be the same. Decide what you want to accomplish and settle on a set of reasonable objectives for the project. Once these are firm in your mind – and, preferably, committed to paper – your next important step is to draw up a plan of your property. The plan need not be a work of art or a draftsman's blueprint; all that is needed is a rough sketch on which the salient features can be recorded.

*The British Grizzled Skipper (*Pyrgus malvae*) is on the wing in the spring. Though shown here on a celandine flower, this Skipper much prefers to spend its time sunning itself on the bare earth or on the surface of a sun-warmed rock.*

Start by drawing the shape of your land, with the main measurements marked in and the north–south direction indicated so that you can prepare for the maximum use of available sunshine. Now is also the time to discover and record other basic features such as the direction of prevailing winds and the type of soil you have to work with. If your property is already fairly well established, you will have to record the position of existing trees, shrubs, lawn, flower beds and so on. Do not – and this is extremely important – do not forget to record where the sunny or shady areas are. Mark any locations where the ground is damp and any possible sites where water may gather during heavy rains. If your winters are snowy, add to your map the spots where the snow lies longest. If you expect frost, show any slight hollows or depressions where stagnant air could accumulate and frost pockets form. All this may appear tedious, but it will pay off in the long run.

While you are engaged in this preparatory work, keep an eye open for any form of wildlife, particularly butterflies, living on or near your land. While formulating your objectives you will no doubt have decided which butterflies you hope to attract to your garden and which ones could be expected to breed there. To avoid disappointment or, worse still, disillusionment, make sure you have taken local advice on the subject and do not set out unrealistic goals for the project. For most people it is best to forget butterflies that require very specialized habitats and to keep to the more versatile species already frequenting the area. If, as may happen, a rare, unusual, or more demanding species enters your territory, then take the visit for what it is worth and enjoy the brief encounter to the fullest.

It is worth remembering too that very few plans of this sort can be followed rigidly. As time goes on, a certain amount of flexibility may prove advantageous. Anyway, with this said let us now move on to consider some of the horticultural fundamentals the new gardener must grasp.

**Clearing the Site** Before you settle down to the interesting work of growing plants that will be largely responsible for attracting your hoped-for butterflies, there are a few mundane activities to get out of the way. This is more likely to be so if you have just moved into a freshly-built home or are trying to convert a rundown property or a piece of urban wasteland, than if you are the owner of an established, well-cared-for garden. For the owner of a brand-new home or the restorer of an old one, the first job, often enough, is clearing the site of builders' rubble, waste products and general trash. While you are doing this, it is good to salvage anything that might be of some practical value later on. Broken-up concrete slabs and bricks make useful walkways, steppingstones, or edging; bits of metal pipe or conduit may be valuable for staking shrubs or trees; an old bathtub can make a small pond; plastic sheeting is useful for creating damp areas; and pieces of wood of any shape or size are invaluable for all sorts of odd jobs around the butterfly garden. Unless you have lots of money and do not mind spending it, developing a magpie's acquisitiveness may be a necessity.

**Fencing the Garden** There is very little point in putting a lot of time, effort and money into a garden or nature reserve if it is not protected from intruders. Also, if the area is to be of value to butterflies and offer a suitable growing-area to plant life, it is imperative to try to reduce the force of incoming winds. Protection can be provided by a wall, a hedge, or a fence of some sort. Here are a few things to keep in mind.

If the property can be enclosed with a dual-purpose barrier, so much the better. I would vote for a hedge over a wall or fence every time. A hedge made up of appropriate shrubs and not clipped to death will not only provide shelter from prevailing winds and give some measure of privacy, but also furnish forage for caterpillars and even nectar for many insects, including butterflies. Unfortunately, a well-grown, robust hedge usually requires fairly deep, fertile earth to grow in. There is no such soil where I live, so if I wanted to grow a hedge, it would have to be planted on the site of a deeply-dug trench that had been filled with good-quality soil. Remember that with a windbreak the intention is not to stop the wind, but to slow it down by putting a multitude of small obstructions in its path, such as the branches of a hedge. A solid barrier like a wall just makes the wind rise up over it and swoop or scoop down onto the land on the other side. But I admit I would not mind owning one of those glorious old walled gardens of England to turn into a butterfly sanctuary!

If you want your hedge to act only as a windbreak, then any locally-grown shrub with suitable characteristics will be adequate. But if you want a dual-purpose hedge, then you will have to give considerable thought to the makeup of your local butterfly population. Around here, bearing in mind that the only clipping I would do would be specialized pruning to promote a thicker, more twiggy growth, I would probably use a mixture of these shrubs or pollard trees: dogberry, withrod, alder, chuckley-pear, pussy willow, balsam poplar, ash and native hawthorn. This mix would give me a good chance of attracting ovipositing female Tiger Swallowtails, Mourning Cloaks, Green Commas, Spring Azures and White Admirals. A British naturalist would probably include whitebeam, blackthorn, common oak, Spanish chestnut, buckthorn and alder buckthorn. Unfortunately, the elm, which I might otherwise have listed, is in serious trouble from Dutch elm disease on both sides of the Atlantic, although the Chinese, Siberian and smooth-leaved elms are thought to be resistant to the disease. Whether or not butterflies found on the commoner elms – the White Letter Hairstreak of Britain, for instance, which oviposits on the wych-elm – can or will adapt to these resistant species as substitutes is unknown to me.

One of the problems with hedges is that they take a long time to grow to a useful size and usually require a fence to protect them during their early years. In this modern age of mobility, the planting of trees, shrubs and hedges with one's grandchildren in mind is no longer the vogue, so more and more people think in terms of wood or wood and wire fences. Such fences are quick to erect and, if built in a suitable manner, are very effective windbreaks. Incidentally, butterflies benefit not only directly, but also indirectly from windbreaks. Plants grown for butterflies grow and flower better and longer if protected from harsh, persistent winds. In my first garden I had a particularly bad wind tunnel formed between my own house and my neighbour's, which were close to and directly in line with each other. This tunnel was extremely harmful to the flowers I was growing. I was hard up for ready cash at the time and could not consider a permanent fence of any sort, so I built a tall rustic frame covered with small-meshed chicken wire directly in the path of the incoming wind. It did not look bad from a distance, or at least I had no complaints from the neighbours, and the beneficial effect on my plants and subsequently on the butterflies was impressive. In a rural or other informal setting, the use of small-meshed wire as a windbreak is quite acceptable, and its effectiveness really needs to be seen to be appreciated. I could, of course, have planted a climber of some sort and trained it up this windbreak if I had really wanted. The line of even a formal type of fence can be softened and made useful to butterflies and hawkmoths by training such plants as hops, climbing honeysuckle, brambles and clematis up and along it.

**Drainage** Good drainage, as any practical gardener knows, is one of the main secrets of successful gardening. Among other things, a well-drained soil warms up more quickly in the spring, and so triggers the early nectar sources into growth sooner and provides a warmer surface for spring butterflies to bask upon.

In areas of severe frosts, particularly without a snow cover, a wet soil will be unstable and inclined to heave if it contains clay or silt, because of the expansion of the water within it as it freezes. This kind of soil will damage your plants and reduce the quantity and quality of their blooms, and therefore possibly have an adverse effect on your ability to attract butterflies. If your soil is inclined to stay wet, you should take steps to rectify the problem. Remember, though, that there is a difference between moist, well-drained soil and wet, poorly-drained soil. The former is good for growing violets to attract laying Fritillaries, and nectar-producing plants such as the primulas and joe-pye weed. Willows respond well to the availability of ample water and are useful for drying up over-wet earth. I cannot think of any value in waterlogged ground within the normal-sized garden. Even flowers such as the marsh marigold and lady's smock, often found in extremely wet conditions, can be readily cultivated in environments that are just moist and well drained.

If you have the problem of too much water in your garden, consult one of the better texts on basic landscaping rather than a gardening book – the latter do not usually address the problem adequately. In the Botanical Garden we receive 150 centimetres (about 60 inches) of precipitation annually, and our clayey soil retains moisture, so we have to make very sure that our flower beds have adequate drainage.

*Like so many others of this group, the Small Pearl Bordered Fritillary (*Boloria selene*) lays its eggs on the leaves of wild violet. These little butterflies enjoy visiting flowers, but your garden must be close to their natural habitat if it is to attract them.*

**Creating Damp Spots** Sometimes a butterfly gardener is faced with a soil that dries out far too readily and allows no opportunity for the growth of desirable moisture-loving plants.

Apart from using the basic technique of incorporating large quantities of organic matter like peat into your soil, you can get around this problem by creating a special environment where the soil can be artificially maintained in a suitably damp condition. First, dig a sloping depression of the shape and size you require, making sure that its depth is somewhat greater than the thickness of your intended planting soil. If possible, the centre of the depression should allow for a depth of earth of 30–45 cm (12–18 in.), and for 15–30 cm (6–12 in.) of space below for broken-up rock. This rock is for drainage, but before you put it into the depression, thoroughly loosen the bottom of the hole to allow for even better drainage. When you have done this, put in the drainage stone and cover it with about 5 cm (2 in.) of something soft such as peat, straw, or fibreglass home insulation. Next, lay in a plastic lining on top of this padding. Heavy plastic sheeting would be best, but if this is not available, a double layer of the thinner material will do the job just as well. Now cut a small hole in the plastic at the centre of the bed, its lowest point, and then fill up the whole depression with a moisture-retentive soil mixture. Once this earth has had time to settle, you can start planting. The underlying plastic will keep the soil moist while still allowing excessive water to drain away. If the hole were not present, you would be creating a bog rather than a damp spot. This technique will work only if the subsoil has good natural drainage. If it is packed, impervious clay, the hole will fill up no matter how much broken stone you put below the plastic – but in this case there would be no need to create such an artificial habitat.

A damp spot can be sited in the garden as an independent environment or incorporated into a larger, more orthodox flower bed. If a shrub, tree or tall-growing perennial is planted so that it will cast some light shade onto this environment during the hottest part of the day, a very useful growing-site will have been created. Remember too that a similar trick can work under a patch of lawn or rough grass. Such a damp site will add further diversity to your garden and may prove an important attraction to butterflies during spells of hot, dry weather. In Newfoundland, for instance, the European and the Peck's Skippers are usually found among dry grass, whereas the Arctic or Checkered Skipper is much more likely to be found where grass is growing in damp ground.

You could create a similar damp habitat by placing soil in a discarded container such as an old bathtub or children's swimming pool. So long as you remember to ensure that adequate drainage is provided, these objects

*Overleaf:*
*The Red Admiral is one butterfly that enjoys feeding from fallen, fermenting fruit. This beauty can readily be drawn into the home garden. It nectars from many easily-grown flowers, and it can also be attracted by old, bruised apples that have had part of their skin removed and have been placed out in the garden. A large clump or a few good-sized pots of nettles maintained near the flower beds will sometimes boost the garden's population of this butterfly to unbelievable numbers.*

should work admirably. You would, of course, be stuck with a predetermined shape that would leave little scope for your artistic flair.

If you decide to try your hand at encouraging the local butterflies to start mud puddling, then you should follow, with some modification, the original basic instructions for creating a damp spot. The whole excavation should now be shallower, with the central drainage hole smaller and the overall diameter not more than about 60 cm (2 ft). It could be filled with a very rich soil kept well watered with a liquid fertilizer made by putting a couple of shovelfuls of fresh farmyard manure into a burlap sack and suspending it in a tub of water. Unfortunately, farmyard manure is not always readily available nowadays, especially for people gardening in a city. For the ordinary gardener intent only on feeding his plants, a shortage of farmyard manure need not be too much of an inconvenience, for there are useful alternative sources of plant nutrients available; but for the butterfly gardener hoping to encourage butterflies to mud puddle, there are no alternatives. If you can't get manure, you must just make do with the saline solution I discussed earlier.

I find that one of the main problems in trying to encourage butterflies to mud puddle is keeping the mixture moist. My locality is known for its incessant wind, which is a nuisance at the best of times but especially for my purposes, because it quickly dries up all the retrievable moisture. I've sometimes wondered whether I could rig up some form of wick that would continually "feed" the mixture with water and so keep it in a permanent state of dampness, but so far I've not tried.

Remember that a mud puddling site should be located in the hottest, sunniest part of the garden. Its surroundings should be clear of any but the shortest vegetation so that the butterflies have unobstructed flightways both in and out of the location as well as room to flutter freely around the attractant.

**Other Attractants** There are some other methods of providing sustenance for visiting butterflies.

Earlier I mentioned that certain butterflies, especially some of the Nymphalids, are attracted to rotting fruit; this is particularly so where fruit trees have always been grown and butterflies have become accustomed to this form of nourishment. There are places, particularly in northern areas such as my own, where fruit trees are rare and sightings of butterflies imbibing fruit juices therefore unusual. However, by deliberately bruising a few apples, allowing them to ferment, and then placing them around the garden, it is sometimes possible, even here, to attract butterflies. I haven't done this more than a few times, but I have had some of the local Red Admirals enjoy my offerings, and feel sure there's potential for the hobbyist in this technique. In his interesting book *The Wildlife Gardener*, John V. Dennis mentions that he has had good success attracting butterflies with a concoction of fermented fruit, sugar and a drop of wine or beer. He mentions among the species attracted, the Red Admiral, the Question Mark, the Wood Nymph, the Red Spotted Purple and the Mourning Cloak. Those of us who haven't already done so, should try this technique at the earliest opportunity.

Some of the Nymphalids can be attracted to a honey solution somewhat in the manner that hummingbirds can be attracted into a garden. The solution, 5% honey and 95% water, is placed in a glass or plastic vial and hung among the flowers where butterflies are working. The open end is plugged with a large wad of good-quality cotton wool that both sucks up the solution like a lamp wick and provides a landing pad on which the butterfly can settle to feed. Some enthusiasts surround the feeding pad with a flower head made of hand-coloured cut-out paper, in the hope that the bait will be even more attractive. Many writers recommend a 10% solution, but though this will be eagerly sucked up by the butterflies, there is some evidence that a solution with more than 5% honey will render male butterflies infertile. This of course is not what we want to do!

Butterflies sense this liquid food with their feet, so as long as the pad is damp when they land on it, they will uncoil their probosces, start probing and begin to feed. For those butterflies fond of tree sap, it may pay you to replace the honey in the mixture with maple syrup – but maple syrup is perhaps not as readily available to butterfly enthusiasts in other countries as it is in Canada. I have often wondered whether different types of honey would prove of differing attractiveness either to specific butterflies or at different seasons of the year. It would be interesting to try an experiment with a few kinds, heather, clover and goldenrod honey, for instance. They taste different to us humans, and some of us have definite preferences, so why not butterflies?

**Soil in the Garden** "Soil" is a common word used to describe what in fact is a very complex mixture of mineral and organic materials and living forms. There are some excellent texts available devoted to the subject of soil. My sole interest in it as a butterfly gardener is whether or not it will produce the plants I want in a condition suitable for butterflies.

It does help, however, to have a basic knowledge of the factors that make a soil suitable for plant production. A useful soil should be made up of 50% solids and 50% pore space. You can't, of course, see the pores, but they should be there, and half of them should be filled with moisture and the other half with air. Only a well-structured, friable soil will be in this condition. Since a compacted or poorly-structured earth has had its pore space destroyed, it should be avoided by all gardeners whether they are interested in butterflies or not. So one of the first things you must do when planning your garden is to check the condition of its soil. If you have a newly-built house in a typical modern subdivision, it is safe to bet that the surrounding topsoil, if there is any left on the site, will be well and truly compacted. If it hasn't, or if you are starting to attract butterflies in an established garden with a well-structured loam, count your blessings.

Any compacted soil should first be broken up into a fine tilth. Unless it is good-quality earth only suffering from abuse, it will more than likely need a large quantity of organic matter mixed into it. This organic matter can be in the form of old farmyard manure, leaf mould, garden compost, shredded peat, rotten hay or straw, coarse sawdust, or just about anything that will decompose without driving your neighbours from their homes or causing an officer from the local department of health to visit you. I once had a large quantity of spent hops from the local brewery dumped into my back garden. I hadn't thought things through very clearly; though spent hops are a useful soil conditioner, they also smell to high heaven and attract every bluebottle fly from far and wide. Since the arrival of my hops coincided with a spell of particularly fine, warm weather, the type you usually associate with lawn chairs and tea outside on the patio, I suddenly became unpopular, to say the least.

My soil has a high proportion of clay and so compacts very easily. I therefore also mix in coarse sand and take care that it doesn't become trampled, especially when wet. It is always wise to stay off wet soil. Furthermore, whenever you work on a flower bed, it is good practice to walk on pieces of board that will distribute your weight over a larger area. By doing so you lessen the possibility of the soil's becoming compacted and eliminate the need to be continually breaking up the earth between your plants. If you have enough space in your flower beds, a more efficient practice is to place permanent steppingstones where you find yourself walking most often.

If you are already a gardener, you will be well aware that different groups of plants require different types of soil. The usual approach in the home garden is to construct a variety of growing-areas, each of which has its own soil and plant community. Typical examples are the rock garden, the perennial border, the peat bed, the vegetable plot and the spaces for shrubs or annual flowers. Though the ground in each of these sites will have a different composition or texture, all must be well structured, and none must be allowed to become compacted.

Though the butterfly gardener with only a small plot under cultivation may plan and maintain it as a replica of a woodland glade, the gardener with a larger property will in all likelihood have several different beds, each with its own characteristic plant community. If you have the space, such plant diversity is extremely valuable.

A good growing-soil must also have its resident population of microscopic plant and animal life – in other words, it must be alive. Such a soil has a good feel and smell to it; if you see one of your visitors casually scoop up a handful and absent-mindedly feel it and smell it, you'll know there's either an experienced gardener in your midst or somebody pretending to be one! For a soil to be alive, it must be friable and well drained, have sufficient organic matter and maintain a temperature appropriate to the season.

Two related matters are soil acidity and richness. Soil acidity is an extremely important but complex subject that has turned out to be far too bewildering for most of the gardeners I meet. Not being a soil chemist myself, I feel there is a lot of unnecessary mystery attached to the subject. Basically, what you have to remember is that you don't want your soil to be either too acidic, or not acidic enough – that is, too alkaline. In the old days an experienced gardener or farmer tested the soil by tasting it. If it tasted sour it was too acidic, if bitter it was too alkaline. A sweet-tasting soil indicated a good, productive earth. In these scientific times we have more exact methods of testing soil, and the amount of acidity or alkalinity is expressed as the soil's pH. The pH scale runs from 0 to 14, with 7 indicating the neutral point. A soil that tests out at more than 7 is alkaline, and one at less than 7 is acidic. Generally speaking, most of the plants we grow for butterflies will respond very favourably to a soil with a pH of about 6.5. If you want to be sure that your plants grow to their best advantage, you should first have your soil tested, and then get professional advice on how to alter the pH, if necessary. Usually a local horticultural college, university or department of agriculture will be prepared to assist. Failing that, there are soil-testing kits available for purchase at most of the larger garden shops; their accuracy, however, may not be as good as you would wish.

The fertility of your soil, of course, governs the growth of your plants and so indirectly affects your garden's ability to attract and hold butterflies. But there are many misconceptions associated with the subject of soil fertility, as well as an unnecessary insistence on the regular and heavy application of garden fertilizers. Far too many professional horticulturists and popular authorities on gardening have never been able to break away from their unenlightened training in this area. If it is so essential to use chemical fertilizers regularly, why is it that there are people with beautiful gardens who have never been able to afford the expense of such fertilizers? The secret lies in the building and maintenance of the type of good-quality loam I have just been discussing.

Of course, there is a place in the garden for fertilizers; the point is not to get pushed into buying and using them out of convention rather than necessity. What sort of fertilizers should be used, and how much applied? I use commercial fertilizers in my work, but I also use organic manures. Natural fertilizers are best, in my opinion, and I recommend their use in the butterfly garden or whenever cultivation is being done with the welfare of wildlife in mind. Chemical fertilizers are wonderful for giving your land a quick shot of the major nutrients nitrogen, phosphorus and potassium, but what of the many so-called micronutrients that are essential to sound plant growth? For these, animal manures and compost are valuable; though they do not usually supply large quantities of the major nutrients, they are extremely useful for providing the required minute amounts of micronutrients. They also add the organic matter essential to the soil bacteria.

Elsewhere in this book I have mentioned the suggestion of some that flowers grown in an organically maintained soil will produce better-quality nectar for butterflies than plants fertilized with commercial chemicals. I have also said that I have not yet found a scientist who believes this. It would be very interesting to know what effects micronutrients have on nectar production and quality. One of these days I hope to set up an experiment to find out.

*Essex Skippers nectaring from the flowers of red clover. If you want this little butterfly to inhabit your land, leave an area of rough grass and wildflowers for it.*

I believe that if the butterfly gardener plants the ordinary type of perennial and annual flower in an uncompacted, well-structured earth, and gives the ground a light covering of animal manure or compost each year, then the plants will in all likelihood be successful.

When I was a lad working on farms in England, I spent many a hard day on the fields lining out piles of farmyard muck with a hand fork and spreading it as uniformly as possible. No doubt I cursed and complained as much as any other farmhand, but when I look back, I realize that the land was in better heart in those days. When the plough went through, the furrows rolled over thick and sweet. Now things are different in Britain, and I sometimes wonder how long the earth can last deprived of organic matter and micronutrients. In North America too we have managed to destroy not only vast areas of natural prairie, but also the quality of the soil on the land that remains.

**Protecting Your Plants** Once your flowers and caterpillar host plants are growing successfully, you must take steps to ensure that they stay in a condition that will attract butterflies. Keeping them healthy is not always as simple as it sounds; plants can be damaged by many things, including high wind, torrential rain, insects, soil splatter, weeds, disease and the neighbour's tomcat.

I find wind still a nuisance, even though I have erected barriers to slow it down and always try to site flower beds in naturally sheltered spots. Torrential rain too plays havoc with my flowers, especially the taller ones such as cosmos. Apart from smashing up the blooms, both these natural forces have a tendency to flatten down the whole plant. Obviously you should take steps to prevent that sort of destruction. You can provide a support for the plants in the form of a stake, twiggy branches, a large-meshed net stretched across the whole bed, or one of the many commercially manufactured gadgets. My own preference is to use branches of birch or hazel or alder. If their butts are pushed into the ground around the various flowers shortly after the plants have started to sprout in the spring, the branches will quickly be camouflaged by the growing stems as the season goes on. If you know the general characteristics of your plants and the usual height they reach, then you will be able to place twigs of a suitable size in the best possible places. Twiggy branches not only stop the flowers from flopping down, but also hold them still and so increase their attractiveness to butterflies seeking nectar.

Dwarf plants such as rockcress and moss phlox that produce their blooms very close to the ground can have much of their value to butterflies destroyed by soil splatter. Soil splatter occurs when heavy rain hits unprotected soil and causes the leaves and blooms of the surrounding plants to be splashed and covered with a muddy film. Butterflies will not take nectar from dirty flowers, nor will they lay their eggs on grimy vegetation. Such unhygienic conditions leave the plant more open to disease and increase its attractiveness to slugs. In my garden, slugs have occasionally ruined the creeping phlox for Swallowtail butterflies simply by devouring petals and leaving their slime behind. If you have a small garden but lots of patience, you can keep the slugs in check by hand-picking them in the early evening or on damp days. Once they are picked, either squash them or drop them in a jar of salt water. If there are too many to cope with, put down one of the commercial poison baits. If you do have to resort to poison, make sure to hide it away under an old flowerpot or something, well out of sight of birds, children and the family dog. Some people sink empty tin cans into the ground so that their tops are just level with the soil's surface. They then pour in an inch of beer, which is said to attract the slugs and drown them. I have never tried this technique, but I have been assured that it works and that the slugs die happy!

The best way to stop your plants from becoming splattered by muddy rain is to mulch the surface of your flower beds. A mulch is just a thin covering of some suitable material such as crushed stone, shredded peat, sawdust, wood chips, or lawn clippings. Some gardeners use shredded leaves, but I find them far too attractive to slugs. I use washed crushed stone over the surface of our rock garden, and shredded peat or wood chips elsewhere where I need it. Another advantage of some of these mulches is that they become warm in the sun and so provide a nice clean substrate for the sunning butterflies.

"Weeds" can be a nuisance in the butterfly garden, because they take up space that could be better used by more desirable plants, and also because they rob their neighbours of available moisture and nutrients. However, remember that a so-called "weed" is simply an unwanted plant, a plant growing out of place; to a butterfly gardener it will be something different from the plants called weeds by most gardeners, farmers and professional horticulturists. Even though I run a botanical garden, I don't mind admitting that two of my most valuable plants are the dandelion and the stinging nettle, and that some of the plants most appealing to our visitors are useless where butterflies are concerned, and would be considered weeds in a bed planted primarily for them. Dandelions and stinging nettles are not allowed, of course, to encroach on the rock garden, peat beds and other specialized collections, because in these sites they would indeed be weeds. But in the spaces devoted to butterflies and other creatures, they would be allowed to smother the most famous exotic alpine or steal every last drop of moisture from a spectacular hybrid tea rose, should somebody have been foolish enough to plant those ornamentals there. Since herbicides really should not be used in the butterfly garden, the only way to get rid of unwanted plants is to remove them by hand.

Certain insects can mar the appearance of plants in the butterfly garden. But so long as they do not affect the quantity of available nectar or destroy valuable browse for desirable caterpillars, what does it matter? As I have suggested, if you are aiming at winning a prize at the Chelsea or Philadelphia flower show, there is no point in trying to become a butterfly gardener. Apart from the parasitic wasps and flies that attack butterflies directly, and from the aphids that suck plant juices, both of which I discussed earlier, there do not seem to be any insects, except perhaps the caterpillars of undesirable moths, that actually lower the value of our plants to butterflies. But there are many insects other than butterflies that visit flowers to feed from their nectar. Since there is usually only a limited quantity of nectar available at any given time, other insects may temporarily devalue our flowers by depleting the supply. The group that immediately comes to mind is the bees, particularly the domesticated honeybee. Having hundreds, possibly thousands, of these industrious little creatures working on your flower beds collecting nectar, cannot contribute to your garden's attractiveness to butterflies intent on feeding. But remember that not all nectar-producing flowers are valuable equally to butterflies and bees. Nectar is far more accessible in some flowers than in others; indeed, many flowers have developed in such a way that they attract a specific type or group of insects to their nectar. The nectar in some flowers appears to be readily available to a multitude of insects including bees and butterflies, but in others it is out of reach of all but insects with a long proboscis, such as a butterfly. The tongue of a honeybee is only 6 mm (0.25 in.) long, whereas the proboscis of the Small Tortoise Shell butterfly of Britain, for instance, is 14–15 mm (0.55–0.59 in.). This difference may suggest that honeybees provide little competition for nectaring butterflies, but I think they do, especially for the smaller butterflies with shorter probosces. Also, their incessant activity on and around the flowers is not conducive to the leisureliness with which butterflies like to feed. For these reasons I have always opposed any suggestion that we keep domesticated bees in the Botanical Garden. We do get a few visits, but only enough to create interest.

My feelings about bumblebees and hoverflies are different, because these creatures, generally speaking, are native to our land and so, I believe, have an inherent right to its harvest. I also believe we have an obligation to support them to some degree, because we are forever destroying their habitat or spraying it with toxic chemicals. Also, the larvae of some of the commoner hoverflies are predators of aphids – a definite benefit to the gardener. Strangely enough, I have always had a soft spot for bumblebees; the sound of their buzzing has for some reason always filled me with a sense of security. Maybe it triggers deep-rooted memories of a leisurely, carefree childhood, days I spent in flowery meadows, or on the edge of a rush-lined pond feverishly hoping for a nice fat roach or perch to grab my bait and send the line screaming off my reel.

Many of the flowers attractive to bumblebees are ones they can crawl into and butterflies cannot. Some that immediately come to mind are antirrhinum, foxglove, toadflax and monkshood. I have occasionally seen this last visited by the Painted Lady and the Red Admiral, but these flowers are awkward for butterflies to probe and usually have their nectar taken by bumblebees, which are adept at pushing themselves inside. Some bees and wasps will cut holes in the back of a deep-throated flower so that they can rob nectar that would normally be too deep for them to reach. We have a very nice honeysuckle in the Garden that often has its flowers damaged in this manner.

There are a number of different kinds of bumblebee, many of which have a considerably longer tongue than does a honeybee. It seems likely, therefore, that bumblebees are in competition with butterflies far more than honeybees are. I think we will just have to accept the competition, for there is really no point in trying to save nectar by attempting to exclude bumblebees from the site. I have always had the feeling that in supporting a large, busy population of these insects a garden shows its value as a safe, suitable environment for transient butterflies and the many other forms of local wildlife.

**Pruning for Butterflies** Trees and shrubs in the butterfly garden should be pruned not simply because pruning is a recommended and worthwhile horticultural practice, but because it is a means of improving the browse for caterpillars and of encouraging nectar-producing flowers. We prune not to form perfectly-shaped, healthy specimens, but to create plants that will provide the maximum possible benefit to our butterflies – although any activity that will assist a plant's healthy, vigorous growth is of course beneficial from all points of view. With this in mind, first cut out and remove any dead, dying, or diseased branches. Then, in order to allow sufficient light and air to penetrate the whole plant, remove any branches or twigs that are growing inwards. These measures by themselves should greatly improve the plant's future performance by inducing the growth of healthy new wood and the production of flower buds. If the tree or shrub is being grown purely as a possible host, then they will probably suffice. Occasionally, however, a shrub is left with only a few whippy stems. These you should encourage to fill out by pruning off a length from the tip of each branch just above a side shoot or bud. This technique should result in bushier twigs that, along with the new shoots that should sprout up from the base because the dead wood has been removed, will provide ample amounts of good-quality food for foraging caterpillars.

When you are dealing with flowering shrubs that produce nectar, it is important to remember that there are two main groups: those that produce their flowers on the current year's growth, and those that produce their flowers on the wood formed in the previous season. Most shrubs are of the latter group. They are pruned only out of necessity and only immediately after they have finished flowering. The fountain buddleia, the lilac, the common privet and the wild raisin are examples. Shrubs that flower on the current season's growth should be pruned and cleaned up as I have described, in the early spring before the leaf buds open. In addition, healthy branches can be cut back to just above the second or third bud on last season's growth; this technique should result in strong new growth and, consequently, large blooms. An example of this type of shrub is the famous

*Overleaf: The common dandelion is a valuable early nectar source that can produce nectar at much lower temperatures than can many other potentially useful plants. I have recorded it being used by eight species of butterflies in our botanical garden. Here, we see it attracting the beautiful Red Admiral and the large, yellow-and-black Tiger Swallowtail. A Green Comma flits past, and a couple of Short Tailed Swallowtails dazzle the onlooker with their dark but exquisite colouration. Though dandelions are out of place in the formal flower bed or lawn, at least a few should be spared, somewhere in the garden, for the sake of our native wildlife in general.*

and extremely useful butterfly bush, which is probably the most valuable attractant for late summer butterflies available to the average butterfly gardener. In Newfoundland, as in most parts of Canada, this bush unfortunately dies down to ground level each winter and so has to be treated more in the manner of a herbaceous perennial. Not so in Britain, however, for there it may develop into a large, sprawling shrub, and is sometimes discovered established in the most unlikely places. Old, wild bushes that have grown up unattended usually produce fewer and smaller flower spikes than those that have been properly maintained. Even so, they provide a bountiful supply of food for the local butterflies.

It is extremely important that all pruning be done only with sharp tools, preferably hand clippers. Save any large, bushy twigs for use in staking your flowers, but burn any diseased material immediately. If you have had to cut out diseased branches, make sure you disinfect your clippers before cutting into clean, healthy growth. Holding them in boiling water will help, but I like to soak them in a household bleaching agent called Javex.

Successful pruning is largely a matter of acquiring firsthand experience of the technique. It is better if you first practice under the watchful eye of a gardener who is already good at it, perhaps a local rose grower. Make sure first to explain what you hope to accomplish, so that your mentor can see exactly what you have in mind and advise you accordingly. Some of the ideas of a butterfly gardener are alien to more orthodox tillers of the soil!

**Footpaths** Garden footpaths don't have much to do with attracting butterflies, you may think. But there are two ways in which they can help draw butterflies into your garden.

Apart from the obvious fact that properly positioned walkways provide access and so allow the gardener to maintain the plants and see what is going on, paths also provide sunning sites for local butterflies. If, as is so often the case nowadays, the garden is small and solidly packed with plants, the pathways can provide some much-needed space for the butterflies to dry themselves off or warm themselves up in. Granted, these insects will use flower heads, the leaves of shrubs, the trunks of trees and so forth to sun on, but usually only when the atmospheric temperature is reasonably high. In cooler, inclement weather when the sun suddenly emerges, the surface of footpaths, being low down and sheltered, will often provide the best place for butterflies to spread their wings and recharge their inner "batteries." Walkways of flagstones, gravel, or wood chips are ideal, for they readily absorb the sun's warmth. If the surface is of grass, it should be kept regularly mown and closely clipped for the paths to be of value. If the paths are edged with natural stones, bricks, or logs, the local butterflies and dragonflies will use these surfaces as sunning sites also. Of course, for a path to be of value as a sunning site, it must be located where it can receive the sun's rays, so bear this in mind when you are planning your garden and siting your tall-growing plant material.

Where I live, we use a trick in building our footpaths that has a significant though indirect effect on our ability to attract and hold butterflies. Because of our lack of topsoil and our extremely rocky, compacted, poorly-drained ground, we construct footpaths in a particular way. After marking out the route and width with pegs and string, we dig out and remove the ground where the footpath is to go for a depth of 30–90 cm (1–3 ft). The depth depends on how difficult the digging is, the number of workers we have available, and whether or not we hit bedrock. Any soil or other fine material we put aside for the flower beds, but the stones we throw back into the trench. When the trench, that is, the footpath, has been dug, we fill it with stones removed from the surrounding flower beds or elsewhere in the garden. We then surface the top with an appropriate material. The great value of a footpath made in this way is that it provides extra drainage for the surrounding flower beds. As we have discovered, it allows the soil to warm up more quickly, to be in better heart, and so to produce better crops – that is, better flowers and host plants for the butterflies we hope to attract. A footpath constructed in this manner is of particular value in an area of high precipitation. If you have very stony soil, it will also give you a way of using your unwanted stones and save you the effort or expense of hauling them off the site.

**Areas of Rough Grass** In the chapter on habitats I discussed the value of rough grass and wild meadow, but how do we imitate this sort of thing in our own gardens? Some naturalists suggest you simply stop cutting the lawn, but I think this advice appropriate only in very few situations under specialized conditions. You could, of course, designate a small section of your lawn as rough grass and stop mowing and fertilizing it, but that would not be very acceptable in a modern city or suburban garden. If you have sufficient space, it is far better to create a rough area off by itself. This kind of habitat must be in a sunny location and, if possible, should be situated on the worst soil you possess. Scientists disagree as to whether rough native grasses and meadow flowers should be encouraged to grow on poor, impoverished soil or on good-quality, well-fertilized loam. From my own limited experience I would choose the former. Many native grasses and useful butterfly flowers like ox-eye daisy, yarrow, pearly everlasting, hawkweeds, asters and goldenrods flourish on nutrient-poor, gritty, acidic earth. Though these plants will also grow on rich, fertile loam, they can become so robust as to be rampant, crowded and impenetrable. Also, in a rich environment many of the more invasive species of little if any value to butterflies will get a foothold and soon smother the more desirable plants. When the ground is impoverished, the plants do not grow as robust or as close together, and the butterflies can move and work among the various clumps of vegetation rather than just within the space at the top. In the Botanical Garden we notice the European Skippers, the Inornate Ringlets and the Arctic Skippers enjoying this relative freedom. Elsewhere I have noticed it with the Pearl Crescent and the Atlantis and the Silver Bordered Fritillaries. Also, butterflies can more readily penetrate sparse vegetation when they are seeking shelter from wind, rain, or midday heat.

On impoverished soil where the taller plants have not created an impenetrable jungle, you will often find that dwarf plants have also been able to get a foothold. Creeping veronica, bugle, vetch and wild white clover are but a few of the dwarf plants of value to butterflies.

To create an impoverished site, you must stop fertilizing, and let the rain leach away any over-abundant nutrients that have accumulated. If you are lucky enough to own good-quality land, it may be necessary to skim off the top 20 cm (8 in.) or so of soil and replace it with rough, inferior earth. In other gardens it may be necessary only to dig more deeply, making sure to bring up a large quantity of the subsoil to dilute the richer upper layer. It is often advantageous to work a bit of shredded peat into the top 10 cm (4 in.) of impoverished soil. The peat will make the site slightly more acidic – which is often desirable in itself; it will also increase moisture retention and so help your seeds to germinate and your new plants to set their roots.

Anyway, if you have the opportunity and the inclination, why not try creating a rough roadside or meadow habitat? Wildflower and grass seeds can be collected from the wild, where collecting is permitted. Remember, however, to take only a few, never all, of the seeds from an individual plant or population. There are now commercial seed firms offering so-called wildflower mixtures on both sides of the Atlantic, but be a little careful of these; many of them have a liberal quantity of non-native species mixed in.

**Wintering Sites** I have mentioned in previous chapters that some kinds of butterfly overwinter as adult insects, and have briefly discussed the sort of protected natural areas they seek out for this purpose. Since many of us are considerably heartened by our first glimpse of one of these butterflies as the long, bitter winter draws to an end, it would be to our advantage to increase such sightings by supplying the local butterflies with additional overwintering sites around our homes. How do we do this?

There are several strategies, and their success will depend to a great extent on the number of natural wintering sites already available in the area and on the number of butterflies looking for somewhere to hibernate. Let's assume that our flower gardening has been effective in encouraging large numbers of Tortoise Shells, Peacocks, Mourning Cloaks, Commas and others to congregate on our land, but that no wintering sites are available. What should we do?

Here are three tricks we use in the Botanical Garden. Our park is large and in a seminatural state, but you should be able to adapt these for use in the home garden. The first, a rock pile, was suggested to me by the sight of Milbert's Tortoise Shells emerging from inside a length of dry-stone wall. Pile up irregularly-shaped rocks of different sizes near fall-blooming flowers or along travel routes frequented by butterflies. Pile them with care so as to create as many inner crevices as possible and yet keep out driving rain or snow and direct, harsh sunshine. Making rock piles for butterflies provides a legitimate use for rocks and rubble that would otherwise require removal elsewhere.

We also use specially constructed and positioned woodpiles. If you build one of these for overwintering butterflies, remember that the idea is to create as many dry, secluded cavities as possible. Therefore, don't just lay your logs lengthways on top of each other – which is the normal procedure – but build up the pile with the layers running in alternate directions. Make sure that the bottom layer is level and that each length of log in it is spaced about 15 cm (6 in.) from the next one. Looking down on it you will get the impression of a series of squares. The third row should follow the direction of the first, the fourth the direction of the second and so on, until you reach the height you want. Before you place the last layer on, it is good to cover the wood with a waterproof barrier such as roofing felt or plastic sheeting. The former is by far the better material to use, for it lasts considerably longer. This waterproof barrier can be tacked to the logs, and then the last layer positioned to help hold it down and to camouflage it. We use 2–2.5-m (6–8-ft) logs from trees that have blown down and are of no other value. In the home garden you must think small, of course, but though you must reduce the size considerably, you can still use the same basic principles.

We make another wintering shelter from pole-sized tree trunks. This one could perhaps be constructed of large branches or, in the home garden, of twigs and small branches that happen to be lying around. We call this shelter a wigwam, because in its general shape it is very similar to the North American Indian dwelling of that name. Building it can be a little tricky. Stand four poles on their ends to form an elongated pyramid shape, and tie them at the top so that their points stick outwards in four different directions. Push or dig the butts of the poles into the ground to stop them slipping outwards, and in this way make the structure perfectly solid. Now, carefully add more poles evenly and systematically around the four main supports, and you will soon have a wooden wigwam. It's surprising how many dry, warm crevices such a structure can offer. In a large garden or a nature reserve it is often much easier simply to tie a support across the gap between two adjacent trees at a suitable height above the ground, according to the length of the poles available. Then stack the poles up against this support, positioning them alternately on one side and the other. The end product is not quite a wigwam, but it does provide a useful shelter. Wigwams are also a good way for the nature reserve warden to store useful timber.

I have seen butterflies fly into both woodpiles and wigwams, but just how valuable such structures really are is hard to say. To evaluate them properly, we would have to pull them apart during the winter and count the creatures we found, and this would defeat our purpose in erecting them in the first place. So I'm recommending them without having scientific figures to back me up. There is no doubt that some butterflies use them, but their value may be governed largely by the number and quality of the natural crevices already available in the surrounding area.

For the gardener working on land surrounded by a formal type of environment, there are some less natural shelters. The first is an adaptation of the common bird nesting box. Instead of a round hole towards the top of the front wall, place a vertical slit 10 cm X 2 cm (4 in. X 0.75 in.) towards the bottom of one side. As with a bird nesting box, the structure should be water- and draftproof. It should also be built with the rough side of the wood inside so that the butterflies have something to grip onto. This box can be placed on a stake 1.5–2 m (4–6 ft) tall banged into the ground quite close to where your late-blooming flowers grow. It should be positioned so that driving rain or snow cannot enter.

*Carefully constructed log piles provide numerous crannies for over-wintering butterflies to creep into. Here a Milbert's Tortoise-shell rests on the pile, while another flies in. A Green Comma suns on the hops that ramble over the logs, as another nectars with a Mourning Cloak from flowers of golden-rod in the centre of the picture. The Compton Tortoise-shell in the bottom right corner nectars next to a Painted Lady, fuelling up before its migration South. A recently emerged Mourning Cloak, or Camberwell Beauty settles on the colouring fire-weed, while yet another sports with a Red Admiral at the edge of the glade. The mice are foraging for seeds, and are of no threat to the butterflies. Were they shrews it would be a very different matter.*

Another shelter of much the same sort is a bird nesting box built without either the orthodox entrance hole or the bottom half of its back panel. This shelter can be fastened, by two 2.5-cm (1-in.) spacers, onto the side of your house, a tree trunk, or a garden fence, with the side with the missing half-panel placed inwards towards the support. Some species of butterfly are adept at locating the flaws in a house's construction where they can creep in and take shelter. This box provides just such a hideaway.

Many of the Nymphalid butterflies take shelter in empty tin cans on garbage dumps or in those strewn around the countryside by litterbugs, and here is an idea for another miniature shelter. It would probably not be a good idea to place tin cans at ground level in your garden, because any sheltering butterfly would be accessible to predators and also in danger of drowning during heavy rains. But if one of the larger tin cans with an end cleanly removed were inverted over the top of a wooden stake and positioned 1.5–2 m (4–6 ft.) off the ground, it might provide a useful wintering site. You could fix the tin solidly in place by driving a galvanized nail through its inverted bottom directly into the stake. You could use a rubber washer or a piece of a car's inner tube between the nail head and the tin; this not only would give a firmer, more solid hold, but would keep water from seeping through the top of the tin where the nail enters. The piece of post within the tin should be small enough to allow plenty of room for butterflies to crawl up and in, and should also have a rough texture to afford them firm footing. In theory at least, any butterfly hunting for shelter would be able to crawl up and find a dark, dry resting place.

Don't forget that evergreen vines might be of value. The English ivy is famous in Britain as a wintering site for that lovely spring butterfly, the Brimstone. Unfortunately, ivy climbs by sending its roots into the surface of its support and so is not very good for the brickwork of a wall or the bark of a tree. Indeed, this plant has the reputation of slowly choking and eventually destroying the trees it climbs. Ivy is not suitable for the walls of wooden houses, and in Newfoundland it is difficult to keep it alive except as a ground cover. There are several deciduous climbers, virginia creeper, hops, honeysuckle and clematis, for instance, that might provide shelter for butterflies in the summer but that would be of little value in the winter. But if you do happen to know of an evergreen climber that survives your winter, it might pay you to grow one as an experiment.

There is always room for new ideas and for experiments. I don't know if my suggestions for homemade wintering sites will work, because I haven't yet tried them. But I hope some of you will; they should bring results under the right circumstances. One great advantage they would have over the rock heaps, woodpiles and wigwams I now construct is that they could easily be monitored to see if the butterflies indeed were using them.

# Planting the Garden for Caterpillars

Sadly, many people still believe that all caterpillars are harmful to gardens. Some gardeners dislike even butterflies, believing that their caterpillars will indiscriminately decimate anything and everything in the form of flower, vegetable, tree, or shrub! The truth, however, is that butterflies are quite specific in choosing plants for their caterpillars. Some will lay their eggs on related plants, but others are specific to one plant alone. Furthermore, most of the host plants required by native butterflies are those considered "weeds" by the orthodox gardener. Destructive caterpillars are more likely to be the juvenile stage of certain common moths than that of butterflies, and the number of these harmful species is very small.

There are times when the population of a particular kind of butterfly, through some unusual natural occurrence, builds up to pest proportions, and the insects become a nuisance and have to be controlled. The best-known example is the Small White or Cabbage White butterfly, which has adapted to breeding on many of our important green crops and causes serious damage if not rigorously controlled. Occasionally one hears of Mourning Cloak caterpillars stripping an ornamental willow or poplar tree, but the tree usually bounces back, and the natural cycles and controls rarely let the situation continue for enough consecutive years to cause any lasting damage. Other examples are the Hop Merchant butterfly's destruction of commercial hops and the damage sometimes done to citrus fruit by the Giant and the Anise Swallowtails. On the whole, however, butterflies are of very little detriment, provided that there is no tampering with their natural habitat and its built-in controls.

It is often very difficult to persuade butterflies to breed in a garden. Even though you provide a suitable variety of the required plants, their

*Commas on hops. If it is planted in good-quality, rich soil, a hop plant will rapidly cover over an unsightly object. Its dense growth and large leaves will provide summer shelter for butterflies such as the Comma.*

positions or the environmental conditions may be such that the butterflies will not lay on them. But if you are seriously interested in butterfly gardening, you will work hard to encourage them not only to visit but to breed and possibly set up viable populations.

If you have the interest and ingenuity, your garden can be landscaped entirely with plants of potential benefit to the caterpillars and adults of local butterflies. Start with suitable trees and shrubs. Sketch out some plans beforehand so that the placement of these does not present any last-minute concerns. In a small garden the trees and shrubs are usually put around the edges and corners of the property to create a woodland effect. This arrangement shelters the property from wind and also supplies a measure of privacy. Only in very large gardens or on nature reserves, however, would it be wise to select tall-growing trees. Tall trees cast shade over a large area and could easily make a small garden valueless to butterflies by diminishinng the ground space reached by sunshine. Only low-growing trees or shrubs should be used in small gardens; indeed, in very small gardens it might be advisable to dispense with trees altogether and scale down your whole operation by treating the taller shrubs as trees. To do well, trees and shrubs require a spacious rootrun in fairly deep, good-quality, well-drained soil. In Newfoundland topsoil is at a premium, and generally speaking, every bit of soil has to be made or at least improved before it is of any use for this purpose. If you live where there is decent soil, you start off with a great advantage.

When you are planting trees and shrubs for caterpillars, remember to leave space in the plan for those trees and shrubs you intend to grow for their nectar production. What species you plant depends on what butterflies are available and what their requirements are – questions you should already have asked, as I have suggested. Always keep in mind that butterflies are sun lovers and that you sacrifice some of your garden's potential with every bit of unnecessary shade you create.

In cooler climates such as my own, willows, poplars and birch should be planted first. All of these families provide food for the caterpillars of many colourful butterflies including the Green Comma, the Compton Tortoise Shell, the Mourning Cloak, the White Admiral, the Viceroy, the Lorquin's Admiral, the Giant Sulphur, the Tiger Swallowtail and the Acadian Hairstreak. The willow has additional value: when it is in flower, it provides nectar for butterflies and a variety of other insects. In Britain these trees occasionally attract the Purple Emperor, the Large Tortoise Shell – an endangered species – and the Purple Hairstreak. Generally speaking, willows and poplars require a fair amount of moisture at their roots. If you have no damp spot in which to plant them, make sure to incorporate plenty of moisture-retentive organic matter into the planting soil, and to mulch the surface around the trunk with a thick layer of similar material. Remember, though, that moisture-loving plants, while they require plenty of moisture, usually grow better if the ground is well drained and not waterlogged. Another practical attribute of the willow and poplar is that they can both be kept as low trees by heavy pruning. Birch too can be cut down and so encouraged to send up numerous suckers from its stump, but this would be a somewhat drastic management technique in the average garden. If you live in a rural area where wells and septic tanks are still a necessity of life, remember that the roots of willows and poplars, if planted in a dry spot, will travel considerable distances for water. They are notorious for clogging up such facilities!

The Tiger Swallowtail will also oviposit on mountain ash, apple, hawthorn, lilac, chuckley-pear and cherry. The common wild pin or fire cherry seems a particular favourite. Unfortunately, cherries, especially this one, are particularly susceptible to a bacterial disease known as black knot, which causes black, rough, cylindrical or spindle-shaped lumps to form on the branches. Not only is it unsightly, it is almost impossible to control without eliminating the tree. Every few years large numbers of wild pin cherry here are wiped out by fire blight, another native bacterial disease. I cut many of my diseased wild cherries down to the ground and burn the pruned wood. The tree usually sends up many fast-growing young shoots from around the stump that will, at least for a few years, provide an inviting clump of potential caterpillar food. But if you have only a normal, modern-sized garden, you would be better advised to plant something other than the pin cherry – possibly the American mountain ash. Strangely enough, my other wild cherry, the choke cherry, does not seem to be affected by either black knot or fire blight. This cherry is less common in Newfoundland; I have not as yet found Swallowtail caterpillars on it, but it is of great ornamental value, and it provides nectar for many insects, including the Red Admiral, the Spring Azure and the Short Tailed Swallowtail butterflies.

The spring-flowering chuckley-pear, or shadbush, would look beautiful in almost any garden. Should a female White Admiral enter your land, it might find this plant to its liking, and lay on it. The Striped Hairstreak also oviposits on shadbush, but this rather uncommon little butterfly is not found as far north as here. It is interesting to note that, whereas the North American White Admiral lays its eggs on a variety of trees and shrubs including birch, willow, poplar and hawthorn, the British species, though it has a similar life cycle and similar tree species at its disposal, oviposits on only a single species, the native wild honeysuckle (*Lonicera periclymenum*). It is much more convenient for the butterfly gardener when a butterfly will visit a variety of host plants, or when a single plant is host to several butterfly species.

The easy-to-grow, extremely decorative northern wild raisin (a *Viburnum*) is the most common host for the Spring Azure butterfly and the Clear Winged Hawkmoth (*Hemaris thysbe*) in Newfoundland. The Spring Azure or Jenny Lind, as it is sometimes called, will also lay on the flower buds of other *Viburnums* and the red-osier dogwood. Elsewhere in North America it has been reported laying on several other plants including ceanothus, blueberry, black cohosh (*Cimicifuga racemosa*), choke cherry and meadowsweet. All are useful for the home garden.

If you live close to nature in suitable countryside, and have a peat bed in your garden, or a sunny corner with a patch of peaty, lime-free soil, you could grow a few bushes of low sweet blueberry, sheep laurel, black crowberry, bog laurel and wild cranberry. These are quite decorative and could become hosts for the Pink Edged Sulphur, the Brown Elfin, the Northern Blue and the Bog Copper. Of course you are unlikely to entice certain butterflies into your garden unless you are situated right alongside their own native habitats. The species I have just named are among these butterflies, but you will not be wasting effort in growing any plant known to be a host for a local or even a less common native butterfly, providing you have the necessary space. Butterflies occasionally get blown around by heavy wind and, like birds, sometimes find themselves well away from their chosen spots. It is always exciting to find that a completely unexpected butterfly has arrived in your garden. How much more thrilling it would be if this unexpected visitor found a suitable plant to lay on, and actually did so!

The mountain alder bush, though by no means a decorative plant – except perhaps in the spring, when it is covered in catkins – is useful because it is a nitrogen fixer and can grow in very poor soil. Like plants belonging to the legume family, this bush can extract nitrogen gas from the air and convert it into usable nitrates. If you look at the roots of these plants, you will notice masses of small swellings, called nodules. These are caused by nitrogen-fixing bacteria that are extremely beneficial to the surrounding soil and make it more fertile for other, more useful, plant life. In addition, alders tend to have a thick, rich leaf litter beneath them. This leaf litter is an ideal growing site for host species such as violets and certain nectar-producing plants such as *Primula*, if the bush is sited where the sun can reach any flowers below it for some of the day. The Green Comma and the Harvester will lay their eggs on alder.

The Harvester is a butterfly not found in my area, so I have no personal experience of it. According to other observers, it is particularly interesting because its caterpillars feed on aphids. Most gardeners dislike aphids because they weaken plants and can render them susceptible to disease. If the Harvester were not so specific in its choice of plant, we might see more of it in the garden – countless ornamental plants become infested with aphids. Of course the controlling factor is perhaps not the plant the Harvester lays on, but the sort of aphid associated with it. There are many different species of aphid, and possibly the caterpillars eat selectively – there is much in nature we do not fully understand. Aphids seem important to the adult Harvester too, for it eagerly alights on leaves or twigs to suck the honeydew secreted by these bugs. Honeydew is also attractive to the White Admiral and Viceroy butterflies, and in Britain to the rare Purple Emperor. As honeydew attracts these beautiful butterflies, perhaps we should encourage aphids in our gardens!

Wild currant and gooseberry can be planted in the garden for the Green, the Grey and the Hoary Commas. If you live in one of certain areas of the United States, southern New England for instance, you could try growing these plants in the hopes of attracting the Red Spotted Purple. This butterfly

*A Pink Edged Sulphur on its local host plant, low sweet blueberry (*Vaccinium angustifolium*), Memorial University Botanical Garden, July 30, 1984. In my area this is a butterfly of burnt-over or clear-cut, regenerating forest land. It is on the wing in late July. It is not an easy butterfly to attract into the average home garden; better to head for the countryside and enjoy it in its natural habitat.*

is now regarded as a subspecies of the White Admiral but is not as limited to forest areas as the White. It visits flowers freely, but whether or not it can be attracted into the home garden I don't know. I suspect that since the White Admiral, an ardent forest dweller and flower visitor, can be drawn into the right type of garden, so can the Red Spotted Purple. Certain currants and gooseberry are suitable host plants for the caterpillars of the Zephyr Angle Wing, the Oreas Angle Wing and the Arota Copper, but thoughts of attracting these wilderness-loving butterflies into the home garden are probably wishful thinking. Managers of nature reserves or countryside parks, however, should keep these species in mind when planning new plantings.

The butterfly gardener should provide certain herbaceous material if a variety of butterflies are to be encouraged to breed. Many butterflies fasten their eggs onto grass or drop them into it. For this reason it is advisable either to provide a special area of rough grass or to refrain from mowing a section of your lawn. As I mentioned in the last chapter, it is better if the grass is not too dense; if you decide to use a piece of lawn, stop fertilizing it and let it starve. Breaking up the surface somehow, will also increase your chances. Wildflowers and native grasses are more likely to colonize disturbed ground, for most find it difficult to establish themselves in thick, dense turf. Remember, if you decide to plant grass for this purpose, do so on a piece of poor, unproductive earth. An impoverished soil usually produces a less dense turf but a greater variety of grasses and wildflowers. Often a piece of bare, unused ground left to its own devices will rapidly become covered over with a mixture of grass and wildflowers. Such a development is often ideal; one has to make sure, however, that some of the more rampant "weeds" like black knapweed, tansy ragweed and yarrow do not take over and smother out the finer native grasses. If this starts to happen, be ruthless in the use of a fork or pickaxe – tear the unwanted stuff out! But though such plants must be stopped from dominating the site, do not eradicate them completely. A clump here and there is a valuable source of nectar, especially for some of the *Nymphalidae*. Encourage as many of the native grassland or roadside flowers as possible, for some may be the required host plants of your local butterflies. The Pearl Crescent, for instance, requires asters, particularly the New England aster, on which to lay its eggs. The Monarch and Queen butterflies require milkweed. Some species of milkweed grow well in dry, grassy areas.

Never would I be without my patch of rough grass, for it is essential to the continued presence of my Inornate Ringlets, my European or Essex Skippers and, to some extent, my Arctic or Checkered Skippers. This last butterfly seems to prefer the grass in a damp site, whereas the others like a drier, more sun-baked turf. British writers on butterfly gardening never fail to mention the value of a patch of rough grass. I can recall many a pleasant afternoon I spent watching Meadow Brown, Small Heath and Ringlet butterflies at the edges of Britain's meadows or in the grass verges of its innumerable country lanes. A patch of rough grass is an important habitat on both sides of the Atlantic.

Grasses and sedges grow among the sphagnum mosses and ericaceous shrubs of our northern boglands. I have two such places on the land under my care, but these are not really habitats you could create in a back garden. Here on these grasses the elusive Jutta Arctic butterfly lays its eggs. This is a large, chocolate-brown butterfly, unusual in that it takes two years to develop from egg to adult, with the adult usually appearing only in years ending in an even number, at least around here. Though I have seen it pass over my semiformal gardens a couple of times, I have never yet been able to attract it down onto a flower bed.

As I mentioned at the beginning of this chapter, many of the host plants for butterflies are considered weeds. Good examples are the Canada or creeping thistle and the European stinging nettle, both of which are important to butterflies, the former to the Painted Lady and the latter to the Red Admiral and the Milbert's Tortoise Shell. The stinging nettle is a valuable plant on both sides of the Atlantic. In Britain it is host to five species of butterfly, particularly the beautiful Peacock. There is no doubt, however, that both of these plants can become extremely annoying pests to the gardener or farmer.

In Newfoundland the Painted Lady's chief host plant is the Canada thistle. Fortunately, in the Botanical Garden we have found that this butterfly will readily oviposit on borage and viper's bugloss, both colourful annuals we regularly grow for their attractiveness to bumblebees. We have not found a similar substitute for the European stinging nettle, which we grow next to certain flower beds to provide breeding nurseries for our Red Admirals and our Milbert's Tortoise Shells, and, with luck some day, for certain of our rare Angle Wings such as the Question Mark, the Hop Merchant and the Satyr Angle Wing.

If you grow the stinging nettle, you should cut it down as it becomes older, before its seeds have a chance to ripen. But this advice is not as practical as it may sound, because the plants, particularly the seed heads, could contain innumerable butterfly larvae. If the nettle patch is small, only the unripened seed heads need be cut off, and then they can be placed among the nettle foliage so that any larvae in them can transfer to the growing leaves. Mowing these plants is a valuable management procedure. A large nettle patch is better mown in sections, one by one in rotation throughout the growing-season. Nettle-associated butterflies prefer young, succulent growth on which to oviposit, and their growing larvae will avoid eating old, coarse foliage, if possible. If planned with butterflies in mind, rotational mowing throughout the season will ensure that there are always young nettles available next to the older plants. Because adult butterflies prefer to use edge zones, mowing wide walkways and cutting out clearings or "bays" into large nettle beds will go a long way towards attracting greater numbers of butterflies; and nettles growing in a warm, sheltered hollow are particularly attractive.

There are many butterflies in both Britain and North America that depend on violets for breeding. If these, usually Fritillaries, are visitors to your garden, it would be advantageous to increase the number of violets available. Generally speaking, violets prefer a moist soil and a little shade to protect them from the hottest sun, so take this preference into account when you are choosing a planting site. Beneath the canopy of an alder shrub would be one such area. Most Fritillaries associated with violets lay their eggs directly onto the plant. However, as I mentioned earlier, the odd one, the Silver Washed Fritillary of Britain for instance, lays its eggs away from the host plant, in this case in a crack in the rough bark of a nearby tree. Should you live in Britain and be lucky enough to have this butterfly visiting in your district, remember to locate your violets close by a tree trunk, preferably oak, ash, or birch, where any larvae will find them.

As I discussed in the last chapter, moist soil for violets or other damp-ground-loving plants can be created and maintained on particularly dry sites by excavating a saucer-shaped depression 15–30 cm (6–12 in.) below the level of the soil surface, and then lining it with polyethylene sheeting. A prepared soil mixture can then be placed in the depression and kept well watered. Remember, it is important to have a hole in the centre of the plastic sheet for drainage, or you will create a bog instead of a moist site! Were I living in the part of Britain frequented by that beautiful little butterfly, the Orange Tip, I would try to attract it by planting lady's smock in just such a site. But this butterfly will also lay its eggs on rockcress, a commonly-grown rock garden plant. Rockcress blooms early and so provides a source of nectar for butterflies on the wing before many other flowers are blooming. It is a useful, easy-to-grow, early nectar source for butterflies on both sides of the Atlantic.

Many home gardeners maintain a vegetable patch. Though the primary intention is usually to produce vegetables for the family's consumption, such a plot can be a useful addition to the butterfly garden. Unfortunately, most people who think of vegetable gardens and butterflies, think of the depredation caused by the Small White or Cabbage White butterfly. I believe that this depredation is the main reason for the animosity towards butterflies in general that can still be encountered in unenlightened gardening circles. I enjoy seeing the occasional Small White butterfly around the flower beds, but I would not suggest it be deliberately encouraged into your vegetable garden. Its caterpillars will do tremendous damage to cabbages and other brassica if they are not rigorously controlled. As I have mentioned, the females of the species will not lay their eggs on dust-covered foliage, so some country people protect their cabbages with a light dusting of flour at the height of the Small White season.

Whenever I think of vegetable gardens in relation to butterflies, my mind seems to gravitate towards that spectacular group, the Swallowtails. The Eastern Black Swallowtail, the Anise Swallowtail and the Short Tailed Swallowtail will all oviposit on the foliage of certain root crops and culinary herbs. Carrots, parsnip, celery, parsley, lovage, dill and fennel are all plants likely to attract Swallowtails. I maintain a large clump of perennial lovage in the corner of our vegetable plot, and every year grow a short row of parsnip, both in order to attract the occasional Short Tailed Swallowtail. Providing they are not present in large numbers, the caterpillars do very little damage to any of these crops. Herbs such as parsley have a luxurious growth that seems to benefit from the regular removal of a few stems of foliage, whether by the gardener or by the odd caterpillar. Root crops too can withstand the loss of much of their foliage without any noticeable adverse effect.

If a few suitable flowers are grown intermixed with the vegetables, so much the better. They will assist in tempting passing butterflies to accept the garden as part of their living space. Female butterflies are quite thorough in searching for suitable plants on which to lay. When engaged in this activity they can be seen quartering the area, touching various plants with their feet in an attempt to find the ones they require. Many butterflies appear to sense the presence of suitable food or host plants through the feet of their back legs, though their sense of smell is undoubtedly located in the antennae.

I remember once watching a Short Tailed Swallowtail systematically quartering our perennial border. I was busy talking to a visitor at the time and, knowing that no suitable host plants were present, did not pay very close attention to it. Later on in the season, much to my surprise, one of the gardeners found caterpillars of this species on each of the four clumps of gas plant present in the bed. Though this interesting ornamental plant is one of the caterpillar foods for the Giant Swallowtail or "Orange Dog," I had never heard of its being used by the Short Tailed Swallowtail. The experience showed me once again that there is always something new to see or discover, and that it is most unwise to allow oneself to become complacent!

Butterflies that are permanent residents of an area have adapted to the local flora. It is more appropriate, therefore, to cultivate the host plants found in the local flora than to try to discover exotic substitutes. Even so, there are a few exotic ornamentals that can provide the necessary caterpillar food for some species. I have already mentioned that the Painted Lady will lay on borage and viper's bugloss, and I can add to these, musk mallow, sidalcea, lupine and alkanet. The American Painted Lady will readily lay its eggs on dusty miller, an ornamental bedding plant especially popular for gardens situated close to the sea.

It should now be clear that if you are to persuade butterflies to breed in your area, above all you must have local knowledge – knowledge of what butterflies are to be found or might be expected to turn up; knowledge of the type of host plant preferred; and knowledge of any alternative plants worth growing. Knowledge of the plant's growing requirements is, of course, essential. You must also have patience and, last but by no means least, that elusive phenomenon, luck.

*The Milbert's Tortoise Shell will freely visit suitable flowers in the home garden, and will often breed there if its main host plant, the stinging nettle, is present. Where this butterfly is common, it can sometimes be seen in the dozens nectaring from the flowers of the Canada thistle.*

When planning your butterfly garden, one of the things you can do is to make up a chart showing the butterflies occurring in your area and the plants they are known to lay their eggs on. This will give you a quick reference guide to the types of plants you might cultivate for the various butterflies you like. The following chart is an example. It shows the butterflies recorded within the boundaries of the Botanical Garden, along with most of their recognized host plants, including those they actually use in the garden.

Making up a chart like this is a good activity for a rainy day. The format makes it very easy for you to add any new information you discover.

## Butterflies recorded from the Memorial University Botanical Garden and their Host Plants

X = Host plants used in the Memorial University Botanical Garden

O = Additional host plants known to be used elsewhere in Newfoundland or North America.

The six butterflies with all "O's" in their column are not known to breed in the Botanical Garden.

| | Short Tailed Swallowtail | Canadian Tiger Swallowtail | Pink Edged Sulphur | Clouded Sulphur | European Cabbage Butterfly | Monarch | Inornate Ringlet | McIsaac's Ringlet | Jutta Arctic | Atlantis Fritillary | Pearl Crescent | Compton Tortoise Shell | Mourning Cloak | Milbert's Tortoise Shell | Red Admiral | Painted Lady | American Painted Lady | Green Comma | Hop Merchant | White Admiral | Brown Elfin | Bog Copper | Spring Azure | Northern Blue | Arctic Skipper | European Skipper |
|---|---|---|---|---|---|---|---|---|---|---|---|---|---|---|---|---|---|---|---|---|---|---|---|---|---|---|
| Mountain Alder (*Alnus crispa*) | | | | | | | | | | | | | | | | | | O | | | | | | | | |
| Hollyhock (*Althaea rosea*) | | | | | | | | | | | | | | | | O | | | | | | | | | | |
| Wild Pear (*Amelanchier bartramiana*) | | X | | | | | | | | | | | | | | | | | | X | | | | | | |
| Pearly Everlasting (*Anaphalis margaritacea*) | | | | | | | | | | | | | | | | O | O | | | | | | | | | |
| Alkanet (*Anchusa sp*) | | | | | | | | | | | | | | | | O | | | | | | | | | | |
| Angelica (*Angelica sp*) | X | | | | | | | | | | | | | | | | | | | | | | | | | |
| Celery (*Apium graveolens*) | X | | | | | | | | | | | | | | | | | | | | | | | | | |
| Burdock (*Arctium sp*) | | | | | | | | | | | | | | | | O | | | | | | | | | | |
| Wormwood (*Artemisia sp*) | | | | | | | | | | | | | | | | O | O | | | | | | | | | |
| Dusty Miller (*Artemisia stelleriana*) | | | | | | | | | | | | | | | | | O | | | | | | | | | |
| Milkweeds (*Asclepias spp*) | | | | | | O | | | | | | | | | | | | | | | | | | THIS IS STILL UNKNOWN | | |
| Aster (*Aster novae angliae*) | | | | | | | | | | | O | | | | | | | | | | | | | | | |
| Birch (*Betula spp*) | | O | | | | | | | | | | O | | | | | | X | | | | | | | | |
| False Nettle (*Boehmeria cylindrica*) | | | | | | | | | | | | | | | O | | | | O | | | | | | | |
| Borage (*Borage officinalis*) | | | | | | | | | | | | | | | | X | O | | | | | | | | | |
| Hackberry (*Celtis occidentalis*) | | | | | | | | | | | | | O | | | | | | | | | | | | | |
| Knapweed (*Centaurea nigra*) | | | | | | | | | | | | | | | | O | | | | | | | | | | |
| Thistle (*Cirsium spp*) | | | | | | | | | | | | | | | | X | | | | | | | | | | |
| Hemlock Parsley (*Conioselinum chinense*) | O | | | | | | | | | | | | | | | | | | | | | | | | | |
| Red-osier Dogwood (*Cornus stolonifera*) | | | | | | | | | | | | | | | | | | | | | | | X | | | |

| Host plant | Short Tailed Swallowtail | Canadian Tiger Swallowtail | Pink Edged Sulphur | Clouded Sulphur | European Cabbage Butterfly | Monarch | Inornate Ringlet | McIsaac's Ringlet | Jutta Arctic | Atlantis Fritillary | Pearl Crescent | Compton Tortoise Shell | Mourning Cloak | Milbert's Tortoise Shell | Red Admiral | Painted Lady | American Painted Lady | Green Comma | Hop Merchant | White Admiral | Brown Elfin | Bog Copper | Spring Azure | Northern Blue | Arctic Skipper | European Skipper |
|---|---|---|---|---|---|---|---|---|---|---|---|---|---|---|---|---|---|---|---|---|---|---|---|---|---|---|
| thorn (*Crataegus spp*) | | X | | | | | | | | | | | | | | | | | | O | | | | THE HOST PLANT FOR THE NEWFOUNDLAND SUBSPECIES OF THIS BUTTERFLY IS STILL UNKNOWN | | |
| bage & Mustards (*Cruciferae spp*) | | | | | X | | | | | | | | | | | | | | | | | | | | | |
| rot (*Daucus carota sativa*) | X | | | | | | | | | | | | | | | | | | | | | | | | | |
| Plant (*Dictamnus albus*) | X | | | | | | | | | | | | | | | | | | | | | | | | | |
| r's Bugloss (*Echium plantagineum*) | | | | | | | | | | | | | | | | X | | | | | | | | | | |
| te Ash (*Fraxinus americana*) | | X | | | | | | | | | | | | | | | | | | | | | | | | |
| Parsnip (*Heracleum maximum*) | X | | | | | | | | | | | | | | | | | | | | | | | | | |
| (*Humulus lupulus*) | | | | | | | | | | | | | | | | O | | | O | | | | | | | |
| ep Laurel (*Kalmia angustifolia*) | | | | | | | | | | | | | | | | | | | | | X | | | | | |
| den Lovage (*Ligusticum officinale*) | X | | | | | | | | | | | | | | | | | | | | | | | | | |
| tch Lovage (*Ligusticum scothicum*) | X | | | | | | | | | | | | | | | | | | | | | | | | | |
| in (*Lupinus polyphyllus*) | | | | O | | | | | | | | | | | | O | | | | | | | | | | |
| le (*Malus baccatta. M.* "Makamik") | | X | | | | | | | | | | | | | | | | | | | | | | | | |
| sk Mallow (*Malva moschata*) | | | | | | | | | | | | | | | | X | O | | | | | | | | | |
| lfa (*Medicago sativa*) | | | | O | | | | | | | | | | | | | | | | | | | | | | |
| Parsnip (*Pastinaca sativa*) | X | | | | | | | | | | | | | | | | | | | | | | | | | |
| den Parsnip (*Pastinaca sativa var sativa hortensis*) | X | | | | | | | | | | | | | | | | | | | | | | | | | |
| led Parsley (*Petroselinum crispum*) | X | | | | | | | | | | | | | | | | | | | | | | | | | |
| lars (*Populus alba, P. balsamifera*) | | | | | | | | | | | | O | X | | | | | | | O | | | | | | |
| nbling Aspen (*Populus tremuloides*) | | X | | | | | | | | | | | | | | | | | | O | | | | | | |
| Cherry (*Prunus pensylvanica*) | | X | | | | | | | | | | | | | | | | | | | | | | | | |
| ke Cherry (*Prunus virginiana*) | | | | | | | | | | | | | | | | | | | | X | | | O | | | |
| rants & Gooseberry (*Ribes spp*) | | | | | | | | | | | | | | | | | | O | | | | | | | | |
| ow (*Salix spp*) | | X | | | | | | | | | | O | X | | | | | O | | O | | | | | | |
| rie Mallow (*Sidalcea malvaeflora*) | | | | | | | | | | | | | | | | O | | | | | | | | | | |
| untain Ash (*Sorbus americana*) | | X | | | | | | | | | | | | | | | | | | | | | | | | |
| adowsweet (*Spiraea latifolia*) | | | | | | | | | | | | | | | | | | | | | | | O | | | |
| swood (*Tilia americana*) | | O | | | | | | | | | | | | | | | | | | O | | | | | | |
| ver (*Trifolium spp*) | | | | O | | | | | | | | | | | | | | | | | | | | | | |
| (*Ulmus spp*) | | | | | | | | | | | | | O | | | | | | O | | | | | | | |
| tles (*Urtica dioica, U. gracilis*) | | | | | | | | | | | | | | X | X | | | | O | | | | | | | |
| eberries (*Vaccinium angustifolium*) | | | X | | | | | | | | | | | | | | | | | | X | | | | | |
| d Cranberry (*Vaccinium macrocarpon*) | | | | | | | | | | | | | | | | | | | | | | O | | | | |
| shberry (*Vaccinium oxycoccus*) | | | | | | | | | | | | | | | | | | | | | | X | | | | |
| wnbeard (*Verbesina halianthoides*) | | | | | | | | | | | O | | | | | | | | | | | | | | | |
| d Raisin (*Viburnum cassinoides*) | | | | | | | | | | | | | | | | | | | | | | | X | | | |
| nnyberry (*Viburnum lentago*) | | | | | | | | | | | | | | | | | | | | | | | O | | | |
| lder-rose (*Viburnum opulus*) | | | | | | | | | | | | | | | | | | | | | | | X | | | |
| ch (*Vicia spp*) | | | | O | | | | | | | | | | | | | | | | | | | | | | |
| et (*Viola spp*) | | | | | | | | | | X | | | | | | | | | | | | | | | | |
| sses — Various | | | | | | | X | X | X | | | | | | | | | | | | | | | | X | X |

# Flowers for Butterflies

Many of the flowers found in the modern garden or for sale at today's plant nurseries are of little if any value to the butterfly gardener. Though some of the flowers may belong to an appropriate plant genus, they have often been so "improved" by modern plant breeders that they have been rendered useless. Generally speaking, butterflies prefer the simple, single blossoms of the older varieties, referred to by some of us as the old-fashioned cottage-garden flowers. Many modern flowers, though beautiful in themselves, are far too complex and lacking in available nectar to be of use in attracting butterflies. Bear this in mind when studying the subject. For instance, many authors mention the value of marigolds for attracting butterflies. Unfortunately, though marigolds are highly decorative bedding plants, only the smallest, single-bloom varieties are usually worth growing for butterflies. Avoid the dense-headed, double-flowered cultivars such as *Tagetes erecta* "Golden Age" or *Tagetes patula* "Harmony"; use, say, *Tagetes patula* "Naughty Marietta" instead. Naughty Marietta is one of my favourite annual bedding plants because it attracts and provides nectar for eight of the types of butterflies that visit me.

Roses are so beautiful, beloved by so many people, that I almost hesitate to point out just how useless they are to the butterfly gardener. Rhododendrons are not quite so bad, for in my neighbourhood at least, the nectar is taken by the Canadian Tiger Swallowtail and beloved by the Clear Winged Hawkmoth. It is possible their tough evergreen leaves provide shelter for butterflies at night or in inclement weather, especially the leaves of larger, almost impenetrable bushes.

No matter how potentially useful they may be, flowers are of no value until the sun is on them. Butterflies need sunshine. Though a few species such as the Red Admiral, the Spring Azure, and the Ringlet of Britain will venture abroad during dull weather if the air temperature

*The Green Comma of North America is a reasonably common spring and fall butterfly in my area. It is readily attracted into the home garden if there is plenty of nectar available for it. Possibly the greatest attractant to this butterfly and many other colourful Nymphalids is the lance-leaved goldenrod, an easily-grown native wildflower shown here.*

is high enough, very few will feed in shadow or on continuously dull days. I have sometimes witnessed Red Admirals flying or feeding on very dull but humid days and even in light rain, and have often wondered how their wings could withstand the rain. But flowers, to be of any use, should really be planted where the sun reaches them for as long as possible during the day. They should also be placed where the butterflies will easily find them when flying from one area to another. As I said earlier, butterflies are inclined to move along defined boundaries and edge zones, and through gaps between habitats or physical obstructions. Flowers should be planted as much as possible directly on these flight lines.

Plant your flowers close together, but not so close that they smother one another's blooms. Planting flowers closely not only will help to smother out weeds, but will promote the flowers' mutual support, especially in heavy rain-and windstorms. A few well-placed twiggy branches stuck in among them will also help keep them standing. Flower stalks should not be allowed to fall down and lie on the ground, or their blooms could become soil-splattered and so almost valueless to butterflies.

The immediate attractiveness to butterflies of a particular flower or clump of flowers is to some extent dependent on what other flowers are in bloom close by. Butterflies with a large expanse of flowers and a variety of suitable blooms to choose from, seldom gather en masse at one particular source. However, if a particularly good attractant, a fully-flowering butterfly bush for instance, happens to be in bloom, it will lure most of the surrounding butterflies to it no matter what other flowers you have provided for them. In my own garden a good-sized clump of lance-leaved goldenrod in full flower sometimes makes me wonder why I took so much trouble to provide other suitable flower types! But I do believe that the greater the variety of nectar-producing plants you can provide, the better it is for butterflies, and the better your chances of attracting them.

Not all flowers produce nectar of the same quality or in the same quantity, but what governs their productivity in these respects is uncertain. One author has suggested that flowers grown organically produce better-quality nectar than those grown chemically. If it were true, this finding would prove significant to the butterfly gardener. So far, however, I have not found anybody capable of proving the point or any scientist who believes it to be valid. But there is strong evidence that a soil that has had its organic and bacterial content kept up by the regular application of farmyard manure, produces healthier plants than a "mined" soil, which has had applications only of chemical fertilizers. If the general health and vigour of a plant is increased, then why not the quantity and quality of its nectar?

The actual size of the flower may be important to some butterflies; so may the formation of the flowers on the stem. Though some butterflies, Red Admirals on *Veronica spicata* for instance, will work suitable flower spikes, they seem to have a greater affinity for umbellate flowers – flowers shaped like the ribs of an umbrella – or for those, such as the composite flowers, that provide a disc on which to settle. The perennial asters and gloriosa daisies are good examples of the latter.

Planting flowers in bold, good-sized, irregular clumps seems better than just sticking the odd plant or two here, there and everywhere. Clumps are especially valuable if the garden is surrounded by purely leafy vegetation such as that found in many a modern horticultural landscape of shrubs, foliage plants and ground covers. The larger the flower clump, the stronger the scent that is emitted, and the greater the flash of colour for a butterfly to notice.

There is no doubt that not all colours are equally attractive to butterflies. Much scientific research has already been done in this area, but gardeners should still take particular note of what colours seem to be favoured by the butterflies visiting their own land. Not only do insects perceive colour differently from humans, but different species of butterflies interpret colours in different ways. Unlike us humans, butterflies can see ultraviolet, so it is possible many flowers have markings attractive to them though invisible to us. My own observations suggest that yellow, blue, purple, pink, white and orange are the flower colours sought by butterflies, and that not all butterfly species are attracted by the same colour. In some flowers, shasta daisies for example, which are generally described as white, it is more likely that the large, yellow, central disc into which the butterfly probes for nectar is the real attractant.

The poached egg flower, that delightful little yellow and white annual so beloved by bees, is another such flower. The outer part of each petal is white, the inner part yellow. Is it the yellow that directs the insects into the nectar source? I started growing this plant some years ago to attract bumble-bees, but since then it has also attracted the White Admiral butterfly, which extended its range into eastern Newfoundland during the last couple of decades. As far as I am concerned, any flower that will even occasionally attract such a beautiful butterfly has a value in the garden.

No matter where you happen to be, watch for and make note of any flowers that are visited by butterflies. Also, note down what butterflies visit them and whether or not the visits are brief stopovers or prolonged, detailed explorations. Even though a particular flower may not be of any immediate value to you in your area, the sighting may indicate a useful line of inquiry.

Never be afraid to follow up a hunch by trying out something new and different. Remember, however, that since butterfly populations fluctuate considerably, it is always better to grow a plant for a few consecutive years before deciding whether or not it has any real merit. If you live where there are a large diversity and dense populations of butterflies, so much the better. You will be able to experiment and gain useful information far more quickly than those of us living in less favoured spots.

I usually have a few annual bedding plants poked in among my more permanent plantings. They add some bright splashes of colour and provide a few useful flowers to cut for home decoration. Interestingly, I have found relatively few annual flowers that are of value in attracting butterflies. The marigold "Naughty Marietta" is my best, and then, strangely enough, the tall, showy, brightly-coloured straw flowers. Very few authors on this subject make mention of straw flowers. The small annual sweet william "Wee Willie" attracts butterflies just as well as the more famous biennial sweet william, although the flowers do not make such a spectacular clump. Candytuft, pin cushion flower and cone flowers are also good. Of the last, I have found the variety "My Joy" particularly useful. The low-growing floss flower "Blue Mink" is ideal for the front of the flower bed, and the much taller cosmos, with its mixture of bright colours, can be placed farther back and will be visited by such butterflies as the Red Admiral, the Painted Lady and the Green Comma. The Monarch, a rare visitor to my area, has also taken nectar from cosmos in my garden – a particularly beautiful sight. Echium or viper's bugloss attracts three types of butterflies for me, and more important, it has proven a favourite host plant for the Painted Lady and is beloved by the bumblebee, another very desirable insect in my garden. Of lesser importance are Chinese forget-me-not, star phlox, vervain, pot marigold and *Cladanthus arabicus*.

One of the problems in using flowers recommended by others, especially from distant parts, is that there may not be butterflies on the wing in your garden when the recommended flowers are in bloom. In Britain, for instance, annual alyssum, mignonette and cornflower are found useful, but I have not found them of value here. The biennial honesty and perennial spur or red valerian, both highly recommended by British naturalists for attracting butterflies, have so far proven almost useless in my garden. Valerian is difficult to grow in this climate, and the effort is hardly worth it.

Of the biennials I find useful, I would rate the Siberian wallflower the most highly. There is a nice lemon-coloured variety, but I find the deep orange one superior for attracting butterflies. The other, more common wallflowers are highly regarded by British butterfly gardeners, but since these biennials will not overwinter in Newfoundland, I grow only the more hardy Siberian. Sweet rocket is useful, particularly for Tiger Swallowtails, and the little common forget-me-not attracts the Milbert's Tortoise Shell, the Spring Azure and the Painted Lady butterflies. The sweet william catchfly is of less value but worth a place in the overall plan.

The most crucial time of the year for nectar-seeking butterflies is the early spring. Adults that have overwintered, or those of species that emerge from the chrysalis early, are often hard put to find spring flowers that can supply the all-important nectar. Dandelions and the flowers of willow are extremely valuable wild sources at this time. In my garden these are supplemented by the pink and white rockcress, the yellow alyssum and the early heathers, especially *Erica carnea* "King George," *E.c.* "Springwood Pink," *Erica* X *darleyensis* "Cherry Steven,s' and *E.* X *d.* "Darley Dale." The first of

*The Compton Tortoise Shell on straw flower. A sight like this in your garden will remain with you a long time.*

these is particularly valuable for the overwintering Mourning Cloaks, Milbert's Tortoise Shells and Green Commas, as well as for the newly-emerged Brown Elfins. It also appears to be an extremely important nectar source for the overwintered queen bumblebees on their emergence around May 16. There are several early-blooming heathers, all of which could possibly be tried to advantage. Aubretia too is said to be an extremely useful provider of early nectar, but I have not been able to grow it successfully; it will grow like a weed in Britain, but it is very finicky in my part of Newfoundland.

Though many annual flowers have a longer blooming-season than does the average perennial, it is the perennial nectar sources that are indispensable in the average butterfly garden. So many types attract butterflies. Since their clumps increase in size from year to year, they are ideal for adding a sense of stability and maturity to the garden. In some inexplicable way, this sense is, I believe, important to many forms of wildlife, including butterflies. Since perennials are required to stay put in the same spot indefinitely, keep in mind that in order to flourish they require good-quality, fairly rich, well-drained soil. The area for annual plants can be dug over and improved yearly, but once perennials are installed, there they remain, and any soil inadequacies are more difficult to rectify.

So far I have discovered more than fifty types of exotic perennial flowers that will provide my local butterflies with nectar. The majority of these, however, appear to be of use to only one or possibly two species. In the average home garden, where space is at a premium, many of these would therefore not be worth growing – better to grow plants capable of attracting a variety of butterflies. A known nectar source should be rejected with care, however, for though it might attract just one species, that species might be a particularly desirable one, and it would be foolish to ruin your chances of having it visit you. In my experience, of all garden butterflies, the Red Admiral has the most catholic taste. I could stop growing perennial cornflower, bleeding heart, astilbe, golden glow and creeping thyme, all of which have attracted no other butterfly, and I would still have many alternative nectar sources to attract it. On the other hand, were I to stop growing the rockgarden soapwort and creeping veronica, both of which also attract only a single species, I would lose my only exotic nectar sources for the Arctic or Checkered Skipper and the Brown Elfin respectively. This would be nothing short of a minor tragedy, for even the occasional visit of one of these little butterflies to the garden constitutes one of the season's highlights!

Some of the useful garden perennials in my garden are single shasta daisies, purple gayfeathers, dwarf devilsbit scabious, Dutchman's breeches and pin cushion flowers. All the single asters are known for their ability to attract butterflies, but I find that the famous cultivar "Harrington Pink" blooms far too late; indeed, in my part of the world it quite often does not get a chance to bloom at all! Phloxes are good. The dwarf, early bloomers in the rock garden or along the edge of the perennial border will attract Swallowtails and Mourning Cloaks, and the taller, fall-blooming phloxes will pull in such butterflies as the Green Comma, the Compton Tortoise Shell, the Red Admiral and the American Painted Lady. There are dozens of different kinds of sedums, but not all appear to interest butterflies. Only the orpine, the stonecrop and, of course, the showy sedum have proven of use to me. This last type is probably the greatest non-native fall attractant consistently grown in my locality for the *Nymphalidae* or Brushfooted butterflies. In a good butterfly year this plant's large, flattish cluster of pink flowers can be alive with butterflies. Some British butterfly gardeners warn that the variety "Autumn Joy" will not attract butterflies, but I do not agree. The first Question Mark butterfly found in Newfoundland was discovered in a city garden feeding on this particular variety. Of course a particular variety of ornamental plant can be called by the wrong name. Plant nursery people, as well as gardeners, can get labels mixed up and so add more uncertainty to an already highly confused plant-naming system.

Other useful perennials include candytuft, chamomile, coral bells, edelweiss, globe flower, globe thistle, gloriosa daisies, carpathian harebell, Jacob's ladder, purple loosestrife, pretty betsy, sea holly, spiraea, thrift, tickseed, true valerians, veronica, violets, sheepsbit, monkshood and leopard's bane.

A few small trees and shrubs can be grown as sources of nectar. Fortunately, these are also useful landscape plants. All the lilacs are reputed to be good and certainly should be given a trial if you have space. So far, however, I have had success with only one type, a common, old variety of French lilac. It regularly attracts Tiger Swallowtails when in bloom and is without doubt a well of nourishment for the beautiful, diurnal Clear Winged Hawkmoth. The flowering rosybloom crabapple "Makamik" also attracts Tiger Swallowtails, as well as a multitude of bees and hoverflies. Lavender, though recommended for butterflies elsewhere, has so far proven valueless in my garden, yet the common privet, when allowed to flower, shows some slight potential. If your area is favoured with a mild climate, you should certainly try growing some of the different *Hebe*. I have seen such bushes in the southwest of Scotland alive with butterflies, especially Small Tortoise Shells. These shrubs should definitely be given a trial. I have no experience of growing them and so no idea which species or varieties are useful, but in his delightful book *Create a Butterfly Garden,* the well-known L. Hugh Newman recommends these three: *Hebe salicifolia*, *Hebe* "Hielan Lassie" and *Hebe* "Great Orme." Newman's book was published in 1967; whether or not these shrubs are still available is up to the reader to discover. Another author has recommended *Hebe francisana* X *variegata*. There is no doubt that *Buddleia davidii*, the butterfly bush, excels as a butterfly lure and provider of nectar. Any of the numerous cultivars could be tried, but "Royal Red," "Mayford Purple," "Pink Pearl," "White Profusion" and "Peace" have all worked well for me. To see a Red Admiral, a Painted Lady, a Milbert's Tortoise Shell and a Mourning Cloak all vying for the choicest position on a sunny spray of "Mayford Purple" is indeed a memorable sight! Do not ignore the other buddleias. The early-flowering fountain buddleia and the orange ball tree, with its small orange flower heads reminiscent of orange golf balls, should both be grown in any area where they are hardy.

Earlier I suggested that whenever you have a chance you should watch butterflies in the wild. I suggested that you pay particular attention to species of wildflowers visited by the butterflies of your area. One reason is that some of the useful wildflowers lend themselves to garden cultivation and so can readily be incorporated into the overall landscape plan. Indeed, I am rapidly becoming convinced that the serious butterfly gardener should concentrate almost entirely on planting and maintaining wild nectar sources, native or naturalized – no easy undertaking, perhaps, but one that could prove particularly valuable to owners of very small gardens.

These ten plants, native or naturalized here, have been recorded attracting from five to twelve species of the local butterflies: Labrador tea, pearly everlasting, red clover, spotted joe-pye weed, black knapweed, ox-eye daisy, common yarrow, Canada thistle, lance-leaved goldenrod and common dandelion. Apart from the spotted joe-pye weed, which requires rich, damp earth, and the Labrador tea, which requires a lime-free, peaty one, all are readily grown in any ordinary garden soil. The occasional vigorous use of a sharp spade around the clumps will keep most of these plants in check. However, if you grow the Canada thistle or any plant having wind-borne seeds, make sure to cut off the flower heads as soon as they fade and become unattractive to butterflies, especially when adjacent gardeners, parkkeepers, or farmers do not have your enthusiasm for attracting butterflies!

The common dandelion is an excellent nectar source for many kinds of butterflies. These include the Short Tailed Swallowtail, the Tiger Swallowtail, the Red Admiral, the Painted Lady, the Green Comma, the Hop Merchant, the Spring Azure and the Cabbage White. The dandelion is particularly useful because it blooms early in the season and can produce nectar at a lower temperature than many other plants. As with the Canada thistle, it is best not to allow these plants to go to seed.

Pearly everlasting is a tremendous attractant, but only for a very short period. I am not sure why this should be so; all I know is that, though the flowers look exactly the same for many weeks, they are attractive to butterflies only for a small part of this time. This is sad, because they provide nectar for at least twelve species of butterfly around here.

All goldenrods are said to attract butterflies, but not all are of equal worth. The small goldenrods appear to be quite important to the tiny bogland butterflies such as the Dorcas and the Bog Coppers, but some of the tall, coarser species seem to be much less useful. The lance-leaved goldenrod, with its flat clusters of golden, honey-scented flowers, is, however, an extremely valuable source of nectar. As far as I am concerned, no butterfly garden should be without at least one good-sized clump of this plant. I would rate it very highly, as possibly one of the greatest attractants on earth for late summer butterflies. It certainly must produce a very attractive nectar, for in my garden at least, it can "pull" butterflies from the famous butterfly bush.

*The Atlantis Fritillary will visit country gardens in my area, provided natural breeding grounds are located close by. It enjoys nectaring from a number of summer flowers, including the weedy black knapweed shown here.*

*The common lilac is a favourite nectar source for the Tiger Swallowtail butterfly and the Clear Winged Hawkmoth. Both insects are easily attracted into the home garden. This lilac is doubly valuable to the North American butterfly gardener, because the Tiger Swallowtail will use it as a host plant. Such dual-purpose, easily-grown plants are ideal for the urban or suburban butterfly gardener, whose growing-space is at a premium.*

Some other native or naturalized plants that attract butterflies in Newfoundland and no doubt elsewhere are tansy ragwort, asters, pineapple weed, wild white clover, lady's smock, lesser stitchwort, hawkweeds, fireweed, white violets, angelica and wintercress.

Native small trees of use both for butterflies and for landscaping include both the fire and choke cherries and the mountain maple. Small shrubs include leatherleaf, bog laurel, rhodora, blueberry and chokeberry. The British blackberry, or bramble, which is so useful there, is not found in Newfoundland. We do have seven similar native species of blackberry, but I have yet to see a butterfly visiting their flowers. On the other hand, the flowers of the common wild raspberry are on occasion eagerly sought after by both the Red and the White Admiral butterflies. I am not aware if the same holds true for the several varieties of domesticated raspberries. Encouraging wild raspberries may not be a very sensible idea. These plants are such rampant growers that, but for their ability to attract the White Admiral and their delicious fruit, I would be inclined to advise their complete exclusion from the garden.

Willows are easy to grow and are often a good nectar source, particularly valuable because of their early flowering-season. But there are many different types of willows, many of them hybrids and not all of them equally valuable to butterflies. I gather that in Britain the pussy willows – goat willow (*Salix caprea*), common sallow (*Salix cinerea*) and eared sallow (*Salix aurita*) – are the favoured ones. In my own area, however, the species to plant would be *Salix discolor* and *Salix bebbiana*, both of which are locally also called pussy willows! Willows bear their male and female flowers on separate shrubs, and though both flowers produce nectar, the more ornamental male flowers seem to attract the most butterflies. Acquire a male plant if your space is at all limited. One of the easiest and cheapest ways to do so, is to go out into the countryside when the plants are in bloom and mark one. You can then return a little later to take cuttings, when the leaves are out. Willows will usually root quite readily if just poked into the earth where you want them to grow. Newfoundland has some rather nice wild dwarf willows that are ideal for growing in a rock garden or for erosion control on banksides. One, which is not yet identified, has been seen to attract the Brown Elfin, a tiny, very early-flying member of the family *Lycaenidae*. Because of their closeness to the earth, these dwarf, ground-hugging shrubs offer nectar in a nice warm microclimate below the level of buffeting winds. It would seem sensible to experiment with any of these dwarf willows that became available to you.

Even the kitchen garden can be incorporated into your overall scheme. Some of the culinary herbs, marjoram, thyme, lavender, rosemary and hyssops, for instance, are said to attract butterflies, particularly in Britain, but I have had mixed success with them myself. Tansy has attracted the Red Admiral in my garden, but not often enough to make growing it for this purpose worthwhile. The common garden chive, on the other hand, if left to flower, regularly attracts a variety of butterflies. It has attracted six species for me. On one occasion in late June I watched a Tiger Swallowtail, a Painted Lady, a Red Admiral and four Clear Winged Hawkmoths all busily feeding together on a single clump about 50 centimetres (20 inches) in diameter. If it is cut down immediately after flowering, this plant will produce a second crop of blooms, though in my garden this second crop is never as valuable as the first. The *Allium* family is a large one and well worth investigating, for surely there must be other useful members besides the common chive. I always have a few plants of borage around the garden. It is a favourite of the local bumblebees and a valuable host plant for the Painted Ladies.

Not all flowers are attractive to butterflies, but I think I have suggested enough useful ones to get the would-be butterfly gardener started on the hobby. Do not be afraid to follow your own intuition. Anything that has a scent and that can be successfully grown where you live is worth consideration. Any plant you see attracting bees, hoverflies and other insects may also prove attractive to butterflies. If you are in North America and are lucky enough to live in an area frequented by hummingbirds, find out what local plants attract them, for some of these too may attract butterflies. With North America what it is, a vast continent with great diversity of habitats, butterflies and plant hardiness zones, it's difficult to believe all the useful "butterfly flowers" have been discovered and given sufficient trial. No matter where you live, it is undoubtedly still possible for you to discover something new of significant interest to the rest of us.

Here is a list of nectar sources I have found attractive to butterflies and suitable for cultivation in formal or semiformal situations.

| **Common Name** | **Scientific Name** |
|---|---|
| **Annual plants** | |
| Floss Flower | *Ageratum houstonianum* "Blue Mink" |
| Pot Marigold | *Calendula officinalis* |
| | *Cladanthus arabicus* |
| Cosmos | *Cosmos bipinnatus* |
| Chinese Forget-me-not | *Cynoglossum amabile* |
| Sweet William | *Dianthus barbatus* "Wee Willie" |
| Echium (Viper's Bugloss) | *Echium vulgare* hybrids |
| Straw Flower | *Helichrysum bracteatum* |
| Candytuft | *Iberis umbellata* |
| Poached Egg Flower | *Limnanthes douglasii* |
| Star Phlox | *Phlox drummondii cuspidata* |
| Cone Flower | *Rudbeckia hirta* varieties |
| Pin Cushion Flower | *Scabiosa atropurpurea* |
| French Marigold | *Tagetes patula* "Naughty Marietta" |
| Vervain | *Verbena* X *hortensis* |
| **Biennial plants** | |
| Siberian Wallflower | *Cheiranthus allionii* |
| Sweet William | *Dianthus barbatus* |
| Teasel | *Dipsacus sylvestris* |
| Sweet Rocket | *Hesperis matronalis* |
| Forget-me-not | *Myosotis scorpioides, M. sylvatica* |
| Sweet William Catchfly | *Silene armeria* |

**Perennial plants**

| | |
|---|---|
| Yarrow | *Achillea ptarmica* "The Pearl" |
| Monkshood | *Aconitum napellus* |
| | *A. bicolor* |
| Chive | *Allium schoenoprasum* |
| Basket-of-gold | *Alyssum saxatile* |
| Pearly Everlasting | *Anaphalis margaritacea* |
| Chamomile (Ox-eye) | *Anthemis tinctoria* |
| Rockcress | *Arabis alpina* |
| Thrift | *Armeria maritima* |
| Michaelmas Daisy | *Aster novi-belgii* varieties |
| Astilbe | *Astilbe* X *arendsii* |
| Astilbe | *A.* X *crispa* "Perkeo" |
| Carpathian Harebell | *Campanula carpatica* |
| Bluebell (Harebell) | *C. rotundifolia* |
| Perennial Cornflower | *Centaurea montana* |
| Shasta Daisy (single) | *Chrysanthemum maximum* |
| | *C. weyrichii* |
| Ox-eye Daisy | *C. leucanthemum* |
| | *Colchicum speciosum* |
| Tickseed | *Coreopsis grandiflora* "Baby Sun" |
| Bunchberry | *Cornus canadensis* |
| Swedish Bunchberry | *C. suecica* |
| | *Crocus sieberi* "Hubert Edelsten" |
| Maiden Pink | *Dianthus deltoides* |
| | *D. arvernensis* |
| Dutchman's Breeches | *Dicentra formosa* |
| Bleeding Heart | *D. spectabilis* |
| Leopard's Bane | *Doronicum plantagineum* |
| | *Draba azoides* |
| Globe Thistle | *Echinops ritro* |
| Trailing Arbutus | *Epigaea repens* |
| | *Erigeron compositus* |
| Sea Holly | *Eryngium planum* |
| Spotted Joe-pye Weed | *Eupatorium maculatum* |
| Meadowsweet | *Filipendula purpurea* |
| Yellow Day Lily | *Hemerocallis* sp. |
| Coral Bells (yellow) | *Heuchera racemosa* |
| Dwarf Candytuft | *Iberis saxatilis* |
| Perennial Candytuft | *I. sempervirens* |
| Blue Flag Iris | *Iris versicolor* |
| Sheepsbit | *Jasione perennis* |
| Red Valerian | *Kentranthus ruber* |
| Edelweiss | *Leontopodium alpinum* |
| Gayfeather (purple) | *Liatris spicata* |
| | *Ligularia Veitchiana* |
| Twin Flower | *Linnaea borealis* |
| Purple Loosestrife | *Lythrum salicaria* |
| Catnip | *Nepeta macrantha* |
| Wild Marjoram | *Origanum vulgare* |
| Dwarf Phlox | *Phlox douglasii* |
| Fall Phlox | *P. paniculata* |
| Moss Phlox | *P. subulata* |
| Jacob's Ladder | *Polemonium caeruleum* |

| | |
|---|---|
| Three-toothed Cinquefoil | *Potentilla tridentata* |
| Primrose | *Primula denticulata* |
| | *P. frondosa* |
| | *P. laurentiana* |
| | *P. marginata* |
| | *P. polyneura* |
| | *P.* X *pubescens* "Janet" |
| | *P. sikkimensis* |
| | *P. viali* |
| Golden Glow | *Rudbeckia laciniata hortensia* |
| Soapwort | *Saponaria ocymoides* |
| Bouncing Bet | *S. officinalis flora plena* |
| Mossy Saxifrage | *Saxifraga caespitosa* |
| Pin Cushion Flower | *Scabiosa caucasica* "House Hybrids" |
| Pin Cushion Flower | *S. lucida* |
| Showy Sedum | *Sedum spectabile* |
| Stonecrop | *S. spurium* |
| Orpine | *S. telephium* |
| Lance-leaved Goldenrod | *Solidago graminifolia* |
| Devilsbit Scabious | *Succisa pratensis* |
| Tansy | *Tanacetum vulgare* |
| Aaron's Rod | *Thermopsis montana* |
| Creeping Thyme | *Thymus serpyllum* "Montanus Albus" |
| Globe Flower | *Trollius europaeus* |
| Valerian | *Valeriana officinalis* |
| | *V. arizonica* |
| Veronica | *Veronica repens* |
| | *V. spicata* |
| | *V. teucrium* |
| Violet | *Viola* spp. |
| **Shrubs and small trees** | |
| Mountain Maple | *Acer spicatum* |
| Purple Chokeberry | *Aronia prunifolia* |
| Butterfly Bush | *Buddleia davidii* |
| Scottish Heather | *Calluna vulgaris, C. v.* "Mrs. Ronald Grey" |
| Leatherleaf | *Chamaedaphne calyculata* |
| Cotoneaster | *Cotoneaster addpressa* |
| February Daphne | *Daphne mezereum* |
| Spring Heath | *Erica carnea* "King George" |
| | *E. c.* "Springwood Pink" |
| | *Erica* X *darleyensis* "Arthur Johnson" |
| | *E.* X *d.* "Cherry Stevens" |
| | *E.* X *d.* "Darley Dale" |
| Sheep Laurel | *Kalmia angustifolia* |
| Bog (Pale) Laurel | *K. polifolia* |
| Labrador Tea | *Ledum groenlandicum* |
| Common Privet | *Ligustrum vulgare* |
| Tartarian Honeysuckle | *Lonicera tatarica* |
| Northern Honeysuckle | *L. villosa* |
| Flowering Crabapple | *Malus* "Makamik" |
| Shrubby Cinquefoil | *Potentilla fruticosa* |
| Fire (Pin) Cherry | *Prunus pensylvanica* |
| Choke Cherry | *P. virginiana* |

| | |
|---|---|
| Rhodora | *Rhododendron canadense* |
| Catawba Rhododendron | *R. catawbiensis* |
| Red Raspberry (wild) | *Rubus idaeus* |
| Meadowsweet | *Spiraea latifolia* |
| Bridalwreath | *S.* X *vanhouttei* |
| Hungarian Lilac | *Syringa josikaea* |
| Common Lilac | *S. vulgaris* |
| Low Sweet Blueberry | *Vaccinium angustifolium* |
| Small Cranberry | *V. oxycoccus* |
| Tundra Bilberry | *V. uliginosum* |
| Mountain Cranberry | *V. vitis-idaea* |

Here is a list of some of the wildflowers I've seen North American butterflies feeding from. These are suitable for planting on waste ground or other informal sites. Many if not all will attract British butterflies as well.

| Common Name | Scientific Name |
|---|---|
| Yarrow | *Achillea millefolium* |
| Angelica | *Angelica atropurpurea* |
| Bristly Sarsaparilla | *Aralia hispida* |
| Wild Asters | *Aster* spp. |
| Wintercress | *Barbarea vulgaris* |
| Lady's Smock | *Cardamine pratensis* |
| Black Knapweed | *Centaurea nigra* |
| Canada Thistle | *Cirsium arvense* |
| Fireweed | *Epilobium angustifolium* |
| Wild Strawberry | *Fragaria virginiana* |
| Cow Parsnip | *Heracleum lanatum* |
| Hogweed | *H. sphondylium* |
| Hawkweeds | *Hieracium* spp. |
| Striped Toadflax | *Linaria repens* |
| Pineapple Weed | *Matricaria matricarioides* |
| Heal-all | *Prunella vulgaris* |
| Buttercup | *Ranunculus* spp. |
| Tansy Ragwort | *Senecio jacobaea* |
| Wild Mustard | *Sinapsis arvensis* |
| Goldenrods | *Solidago* spp. |
| Lesser Stitchwort | *Stellaria graminea* |
| Dandelion | *Taraxacum officinale* |
| Meadow Rue | *Thalictrum pubescens* |
| Red Clover | *Trifolium pratense* |
| Wild White Clover | *T. repens* |
| Coltsfoot | *Tussilago farfara* |
| Cow Vetch | *Vicia cracca* |
| Northern White Violet | *Viola pallens* |

*Brown Elfin on leatherleaf (*Chamaedaphne calyculata*), one of its few nectar sources. I love this little harbinger of spring. After our long, dreary winter, a sight of this shy little butterfly is a promise of better things to come. Even with patches of snow still in the woods and tenaciously clinging to our flower beds, this tiny creature can, with luck, be spotted sipping nectar from the flowers of the early-blooming heather* Erica carnea *"King George."*

Here is a list of some plants others have found attractive to nectaring butterflies in Britain or North America. Unfortunately, many authors use only common names for the plants they recommend, and their practice sometimes creates confusion as to a flower's true identity. I have therefore provided what I think are the appropriate scientific equivalents of these common names where none were given by the various authors. But these scientific equivalents should not be taken as "gospel," because often a number of plants are known by the same common name. Where an author has recorded both the common and scientific names, I have left these unchanged, whether or not they coincide with my own understanding of the nomenclature. Plant-naming, both scientific and horticultural, is in a state of confusion, and I have neither the inclination nor the audacity to outguess or contradict other authors. Also, remember that only certain species of a plant genus or only a certain variety of a species may be capable of attracting butterflies. And remember that a number of species within a genus may share in common a common English name – thrift, for example. Some potentially useful plants that I have seen recorded elsewhere, I have omitted from this list, simply because the name used was far too vague to indicate just exactly what the plant was. One of the most aggravating problems faced by botanical gardens is how to label their botanical specimens accurately. The problem spills over into all sorts of other activities, and one can really get into trouble trying to put together a scientifically accurate list. But rather than leave this list out of the book altogether, I decided to do what I could and hope for the best – may the botanists and plant taxonomists understand my dilemma! Anyway, the following, though something of a hodge-podge of shrubs, traditional ornamental flowers, culinary herbs and "weeds," should, I believe, be worth looking at. I have not tried to place the non-woody plants in a separate category, because such categorization would open up too much controversy. A "weed" is simply a plant growing out of place; it's up to the individual gardener whether a "weed" is used as an ornamental flower or an ornamental flower is considered a "weed." Remember above all that the best way to build up a collection of valuable butterfly flowers for your garden is to use only those plants that have been positively identified, by reliable observers, as being of use to the butterflies of your area.

| **Common Name** | **Scientific Name** |
|---|---|
| **Garden flowers, culinary herbs and "weeds"** | |
| Corn Cockle | *Agrostemma githago* |
| | *A. milas* |
| Bugle | *Ajuga reptans* |
| | *Allium senescens* |
| Marsh-mallow | *Althea officinalis* |
| Italian Bugloss | *Anchusa azurea* |
| Kidney Vetch | *Anthyllis vulneraria* |
| Dogbane | *Apocynum* spp. |
| Thrift | *Armeria formosa* |
| Milkweed | *Asclepias syriaca, A. incarnata* |
| Aster | *Aster amellus* |
| Aubretia | *Aubretia deltoidea* |

| | |
|---|---|
| Baptisia | *Baptisia alba, B. leucophaea* |
| Daisy | *Bellis perennis* |
| Bergenia | *Bergenia crassifolia* |
| Bidens | *Bidens aristosa, B. cernua, B. coronata, B. laevis* |
| Rape | *Brassica napus* |
| White Bryony | *Bryonia alba* |
| Lesser Calamint | *Calamintha nepeta* |
| China Aster | *Callistephus chinensis* |
| Milky Bellflower | *Campanula lactiflora* |
| Musk Thistle | *Carduus nutans* |
| Carline Thistle | *Carlina vulgaris* |
| Cornflower | *Centaurea cyanus* |
| Brown Knapweed | *C. jacea* |
| Yellow Knapweed | *C. macrocephala* |
| Greater Knapweed | *C. scabiosa* |
| Common Mouse-ear | *Cerastium holosteoides* |
| Wallflower | *Cheiranthus cheiri* |
| Rubellum Chrysanthemums | *Chrysanthemum rubellum* |
| Corn Marigold | *C. segetum* |
| Dwarf Thistle | *Cirsium acaule* |
| Clematis | *Clematis heracleifolia* (syn. *C. tubulosa*) |
| Bindweed | *Convolvulus arvensis* |
| Lance-leaved Coreopsis | *Coreopsis lanceolata* |
| Ivy-leaved Toadflax | *Cymbalaria muralis* |
| Hound's-tongue | *Cynoglossum officinale* |
| Dahlia | *Dahlia* "Coltness Hybrids" |
| Queen Anne's Lace (Wild Carrot) | *Daucus carota* |
| Fleabane | *Erigeron macranthus, E. speciosus* |
| Alpine Wallflower | *Erysimum linifolium* |
| Hemp Agrimony | *Eupatorium cannabinum* |
| Mistflower | *E. coelestinum* |
| Boneset | *E. perfoliatum* |
| Sweet Joe-pye Weed | *E. purpureum* |
| Mexican Fire Plant | *Euphorbia heterophylla* |
| Wild Buckwheat | *Fagopyrum sagittatum* |
| Lady's Bedstraw | *Galium verum* |
| Gazania | *Gazania* X *splendens* |
| Cranebills | *Geranium* spp. |
| Linanthus | *Gilia aggregata* |
| Godetia | *Godetia grandiflora* |
| Sweet-scented Orchid | *Gymnadenia conopsea* |
| Ivy | *Hedera helix* |
| Sneezeweed | *Helenium autumnale* |
| Little Sunflower | *Helianthella* sp. |
| Common Rock-rose | *Helianthemum chamaecistus* |
| Orange Sunflower | *Heliopsis helianthoides, H. major* |
| Common Heliotrope | *Heliotropium arborescens* |
| Cherry Pie | *H. peruvianum* |
| Orange Day Lily | *Hemerocallis* sp. |
| Horseshoe Vetch | *Hippocrepis comosa* |
| Bluebell | *Hyacinthoides non-scripta* |

| | |
|---|---|
| Perforate St. John's-wort | *Hypericum perforatum* |
| Cat's-ear | *Hypochoeris radicata* |
| Hyssop | *Hyssopus officinalis* |
| Wild Candytuft | *Iberis amara* |
| Inula | *Inula ensifolia, I. hookeri* |
| Sheepsbit | *Jasione montana* |
| Field Scabious | *Knautia arvensis* |
| Red-hot-poker | *Kniphofia* spp. |
| Red Dead-nettle | *Lamium purpureum* |
| Lantana | *Lantana montevidensis* |
| Meadow Vetchling | *Lathyrus pratensis* |
| Tidy-tips | *Layia elegans* |
| Hawkbits | *Leontodon* spp. |
| Ligularia | *Ligularia dentata* "Othello," *L. clivorum* |
| Sea Lavender | *Limonium sinuata* |
| Lippia | *Lippia canescens* |
| Lobelia | *Lobelia* sp. |
| Sweet Allyssum | *Lobularia maritimum* |
| Birdsfoot Trefoil | *Lotus corniculatus* |
| Honesty | *Lunaria annua, L. rediviva* |
| Alpine Campion | *Lychnis alpina* |
| Maltese Cross | *L. chalcedonica* |
| Rose Campion | *L. coronaria* |
| Red Campion | *L. dioica* |
| Ragged Robin | *L. flos-cuculi* |
| Loosestrife | *Lysimachia clethroides* |
| Musk Mallow | *Malva moschata* |
| Night-scented Stock | *Matthiola bicornis* |
| Black Medick | *Medicago lupulina* |
| Lucerne | *M. sativa* |
| Water Mint | *Mentha aquatica* |
| Horse Mint | *M. longifolia* |
| Apple Mint | *M. rotundifolia* |
| Wild Bergamot | *Monarda fistulosa* |
| Daffodils | *Narcissus* spp. |
| Catmint | *Nepeta mussinii, N.* X *faasenii* |
| Tobacco Plant | *Nicotiana* spp. |
| Red Bartsia | *Odontites rubra* |
| Sainfoin | *Onobrychis viciifolia* |
| Early-purple Orchid | *Orchis mascula* |
| Sweet Marjoram | *Origanum majorana* |
| Scarlet Geranium | *Pelargonium* X *hotorum* |
| Petunia (single) | *Petunia hybrida* |
| | *Phuopsis stylosa* |
| Rampion | *Phyteuma tenerum* |
| Snakeweed | *Polygonum bistorta* |
| Hoary Cinquefoil | *Potentilla argentea* |
| | *P.* X "Tonguei" and *P.* spp. |
| Oxlip | *Primula elatior* |
| Polyanthus Primrose | *P. polyanthus* |
| Cowslip | *P. veris* |
| Common Primrose | *P. vulgaris* |
| Fleabane | *Pulicaria dysenterica* |
| Pyxie | *Pyxidanthera barbulata* |

| | |
|---|---|
| Lesser Celandine | *Ranunculus ficaria* |
| Mignonette | *Reseda odorata* |
| Black-eyed Susan | *Rudbeckia hirta, R. purpurea* |
| Small Scabious | *Scabiosa columbaria* |
| Wall-pepper | *Sedum acre* |
| Sea Ragwort | *Senecio cineraria* |
| Groundsel | *S. vulgaris* |
| | *S.* "Sunshine," |
| | *S. leucostachys* |
| Saw-wort | *Serratula tinctoria* |
| Moss Campion | *Silene acaulis* |
| White Campion | *S. alba* |
| Bladder Campion | *S. vulgaris* |
| Goldenrods | *Solidago* spp. |
| Corn Sow-thistle | *Sonchus arvensis* |
| Betony | *Stachys officinalis* |
| Marsh Woundwort | *S. palustris* |
| | *Stevia purpurea* |
| Stokes Aster | *Stokesia laevis* |
| Russian Comfrey | *Symphytum* X *uplandicum* |
| Black Bryony | *Tamus communis* |
| Thymes | *Thymus drucei, T. pulegioides, T. serphyllum, T. vulgaris* |
| Clovers | *Trifolium arvense, T. hybridum, T. ochroleucon, T. striatum* |
| Mexican Flame Vine | *Tropaeolum* sp. |
| Colt's-foot | *Tusilago farfara* |
| Verbena | *Verbena hybrida, V. officinalis, V. bonariensis, V. venosa* |
| Tare | *Vicia hirsuta, V. tetrasperma* |
| Field Pansy | *Viola arvensis* |
| Heath Dog-violet | *V. canina* |
| Common Dog-violet | *V. riviniana* |
| Heartsease | *V. tricolor* |
| **Shrubs and trees** | |
| Glossy Abelia | *Abelia* X *grandiflora, A. schumanii* |
| Hyssop | *Agastache anethiodora* |
| Strawberry Tree | *Arbutus unedo* |
| Fountain Buddleia | *Buddleia alternifolia* |
| | *B. colvillei* |
| | *B. crispa* |
| | *B. fallowiana* |
| | *B.* "Lochinch" |
| Orange Ball Tree | *B. globosa* |
| | *B. weyeriana* |
| Blue Spiraea | *Caryopteris* X *clandonensis* |
| Sweet Chestnut | *Castanea sativa* |
| California Lilac | *Ceanothus americanus* |
| | *C.* X *delilianus* "Gloire de Versailles" |
| | *C. dentatus* |
| Button Bush | *Cephalanthus occidentalis* |
| Lead-wort | *Ceratostigma willmottianum* |
| Mexican Orange | *Choisya ternata* |

| | |
|---|---|
| Glorybower | *Clerodendrum bungei* |
| Anchor Plant | *Colletia armata* |
| European Hazel | *Corylus avellana* |
| Hawthorn | *Crataegus monogyna, C. laevigata* |
| Winter Daphne | *Daphne odora* |
| Spring Heath | *Erica carnea* varieties |
| Bell Heath | *E. cinerea* varieties |
| Irish Heath | *E. mediterranea* "Superba" |
| Cross-leaved Heath | *E. tetralix* |
| Cornish Heath | *E. vagans* |
| Escallonia | *Escallonia hybrids, E. bifida, E. macrantha* |
| Alder Buckthorn | *Frangula alnus* |
| | *Hebe albicans* |
| | *H.* X *andersonii* "Variegata" |
| | *H. brachysiphon* |
| | *H. francisana* X *variegata* |
| Shrubby Veronica | *H. salicifolia* |
| | *H. speciosa* |
| | *H.* "Great Orme" |
| | *H.* "Hielan Lassie" |
| | *H.* "Midsummer Beauty" |
| | *H.* "Purple Queen" |
| Sun Roses | *Helianthemum nummularium* |
| Jasmine | *Jasminum nudiflorum* |
| Lantana | *Lantana camara* |
| Lavender | *Lavandula officinalis, L. angustifolia* "Dwarf Munstead Blue" |
| Lemon Verbena | *Lippia citriodora* |
| Climbing Honeysuckle | *Lonicera pericylmenum* |
| | *Microglossa albescens* )syn. *Aster cabulicus*) |
| Mock Orange | *Philadelphus* spp. |
| Nine Bark | *Physocarpus opulifolius* |
| Cape Plumbago | *Plumbago capensis* |
| Wild Cherry | *Prunus avium* |
| Common Laurel | *P. laurocerasus* |
| Blackthorn | *P. spinosa* |
| Wild Pear | *Pyrus communis* |
| Rosemary | *Rosemarinus officinalis* |
| Bramble | *Rubus fruticosus, R. deliciosus* |
| Pussy Willow | *Salix aurita, S. caprea, S. cinerea* |
| Broom | *Sarothamnus scoparius* |
| | *Senecio greyi* |
| Chinese Lilac | *Syringa* X *chinesis* |
| Persian Lilac | *S.* X *persica* |
| Lime Trees | *Tilia* spp. |
| Viburnums | *Viburnum* X *burkwoodii, V.* X *carlcephalum, V. lantana* |
| Chastetree | *Vitex agnus-castus, V. negunda* |

*Bumblebee on cowslips. The bumblebee is another beneficial insect that itself benefits from a butterfly garden. Though it sometimes competes for nectar, it is compatible with butterflies and should be welcome around the flowers.*

ˈlere is a chart showing the twenty best ectar sources I have found – flowers tive to five or more species of butterfly wfoundland. Observations were made ghout Newfoundland, not just in the ical Garden.

| | Short Tailed Swallowtail | Canadian Tiger Swallowtail | Pink Edged Sulphur | Clouded Sulphur | Monarch | McIsaac's Ringlet | Jutta Arctic | Atlantis Fritillary | Silver Bordered Fritillary | Pearl Crescent | Green Comma | Hop Merchant | Compton Tortoise Shell | Milbert's Tortoise Shell | Mourning Cloak | Red Admiral | American Painted Lady | Painted Lady | White Admiral | Dorcas Copper | Bog Copper | Northern Blue | Arctic Blue | Spring Azure | Arctic Skipper | European Skipper | # of species visiting these individual flowers |
|---|---|---|---|---|---|---|---|---|---|---|---|---|---|---|---|---|---|---|---|---|---|---|---|---|---|---|---|
| EXOTICS: | | | | | | | | | | | | | | | | | | | | | | | | | | | |
| Marigold (*Tagetes patula* "Naughty Marietta") | X | X | X | | | | | X | | | X | | | X | X | X | X | X | | | | | | | | | 10 |
| Flower (*Helichrysum bracteatum*) | | | | | | | | | | | | | X | X | X | X | | X | | | | | | | | | 5 |
| Sweet William (*Dianthus barbatus* "Wee Willie") | X | | | | | X | | | | | X | | | | | X | | | | | | | | | | X | 5 |
| ng Bet (*Saponaria officinalis*) | | | | | | | | | | | X | | X | X | X | X | | | | | | | | | | | 5 |
| ox (*Phlox paniculata*) | | | | | | | | | | | X | | X | | X | X | X | | | | | | | | | | 5 |
| *Allium schoenoprasum*) | X | X | | | | | | | | | | | | X | | X | | X | | | | | | | X | | 6 |
| ess (*Arabis alpina grandiflora*) | | | | | | | | | | | X | | | X | X | X | | | | | | | | X | | | 5 |
| fly Bush (*Buddleia davidii*) | | | | | X | | | | | | | | | X | X | X | X | X | | | | | | | | | 6 |
| Sedum (*Sedum spectabile*) | | | | | | | | | | | X | | | X | X | X | X | X | | | | | | | | | 6 |
| n Wallflower (*Cheiranthus allionii*) | | X | | | | | | | | | X | | | X | | X | | X | | | | | | | | | 5 |
| INDIGENOUS OR NATURALIZED: | | | | | | | | | | | | | | | | | | | | | | | | | | | |
| or Tea (*Ledum groenlandicum*) | X | | | | | X | X | | | | | | | | | | | X | | | | | X | | | | 5 |
| on Dandelion (*Taraxacum officinale*) | X | X | | | | | | | | | X | X | | | | X | | X | | | | | | X | | | 7 |
| Everlasting (Anaphalis margaritacea) | | | X | | | | | X | X | | | | | X | X | X | | | X | X | X | X | | | | X | 11 |
| over (*Trifolium pratense*) | | X | X | | X | | | | | | | | | | X | | X | X | | | | | | | | X | 7 |
| eaved Goldenrod (*Solidage graminifolia*) | | | | X | X | | | | | | X | | X | X | X | X | X | X | X | | | | | | | X | 11 |
| d Joe-pye Weed (*Eupatorium maculatum*) | | | | | | | | X | X | | X | | | X | | X | | X | | | X | X | | | | | 8 |
| Knapweed (*Centaurea nigra*) | | | | | X | | | X | | | X | | | X | | X | X | X | | | | | | | | X | 8 |
| Daisy (*Chrysanthemum leucanthemum*) | | | | | | X | | X | | X | | | | X | | | | | | X | | X | | | X | X | 8 |
| on Yarrow (*Achillea millefolium*) | | | | | | | | X | | | | | X | X | | X | X | X | | | | | | | | | 6 |
| Thistle (*Cirsium arvense*) | | | | | | | | | | | X | | | X | | X | | X | X | | | | | | | X | 6 |
| ese flowers visited by the specific butterflies shown | 5 | 5 | 3 | 1 | 4 | 3 | 1 | 6 | 2 | 1 | 11 | 1 | 5 | 15 | 10 | 17 | 8 | 14 | 3 | 2 | 2 | 3 | 1 | 2 | 2 | 7 | |

*ugh these records are from Newfoundland, there is no reason to believe that these twenty flowers would not be of derable value for attracting butterflies in any area where they can be grown and where wild butterflies occur. mber, however, that for a flower to be of any value it must bloom and produce nectar at a time when there are rflies on the wing to take advantage of it. Sometimes climatic and other natural conditions dictate that flowering ns and butterfly flight periods cannot be synchronized.*

# Rearing Butterflies in Captivity

As I start this chapter, I feel I'm being a bit of a fraud, for many other people, especially in Britain and the United States, are far better qualified to write on this subject. But I have reared several species from time to time and don't see any harm in passing on my own thoughts about it. I have not lived in the British Isles for a good many years, and my experience in this area has been solely with those North American butterflies found in Newfoundland. Many of these species, or very similar ones, are, of course, found on both sides of the Atlantic. Anyway, since the basic principles apply everywhere, a beginner reading this chapter should find it useful.

The first thing you should know about rearing butterflies in captivity is that it is a time-consuming hobby, one that requires a great deal of patience and that is better left alone unless you are prepared to do it properly. For your own peace of mind the second thing to remember is that you should at first attempt to rear only the easy, common types. Regardless of how enthusiastic you may be, you should attempt the difficult or rare butterflies only after you have gained considerable practical experience and specialized knowledge. For most of us, it makes better sense to leave the rare or difficult butterflies strictly alone, and to let the scientists, who should know what they are doing, get on with them.

Once you have decided to rear butterflies, your immediate problem is where to get the desired live material. In Britain there are butterfly farms where butterflies in various stages of the life cycle can be bought. Not so, as far as I know, in Canada. Here we must follow the other method of obtaining stock, which is, of course, to go out into the countryside and collect it. I also find it worthwhile to put the word out to the local gardeners, for once they know you are interested in this sort of thing, they can quite often put you onto the track of something useful. You may get bothered by gifts of caterpillars of little interest to you, but every now and again something desirable will be brought in. I have had caterpillars of the Tiger Swallowtail, the Short Tailed Swallowtail, the Red Admiral, the Mourning Cloak and the Painted Lady offered to me, sometimes in considerable numbers. Most of these caterpillars are regarded as pests by orthodox gardeners, and although they don't do much harm locally, they are still considered "bugs" and dealt with accordingly.

Last summer a professional economic entomologist friend of mine had a very sad experience. A small farmer came into town bringing him a Short Tailed Swallowtail caterpillar for identification and asking for advice on what spray to use against such creatures. The man mentioned that the day before he had squashed over three hundred of these caterpillars on his parsnips growing in a small seaside field! Apart from the waste of the beautiful creatures, the occurrence was particularly sad because Swallowtail caterpillars, if well distributed among the leaves, do little harm to parsnips. Had we known earlier, my friend and I would have rushed out and salvaged them. The farm was only 273 kilometres (170 miles) away, a reasonably short jaunt in Newfoundland, and I would have delighted in releasing them throughout the Botanical Garden. We have several patches of the Swallowtail's wild host plant growing within our boundaries, and my wife always cultivates a row of parsnips in her vegetable garden just for this butterfly. She has also left a huge clump of garden lovage, which we seldom use, growing in the corner of this plot, simply to encourage any passing female Short Tailed Swallowtail to stop briefly and lay on it.

It is always best to have your rearing equipment ready well in advance, and not be caught at the last minute without appropriate facilities. The first thing you require is a cage of some sort. This can be as small as an empty jar or large enough to walk around in. I don't like using glass jars, because they heat up too easily, are prone to condensation on their sides, and are fiddly to keep clean when in use. But if you have access to some of the large-mouthed gallon pickle jars, don't turn them down, for they can make very useful cages at a pinch. If you do happen to use a glass container, make sure not to allow condensation to build up on the inside. You can prevent it by keeping the jar out of the direct rays of the sun and by regularly wiping down the inside with an absorbent paper. In general, although caterpillars and butterflies require plenty of sunlight, it is bad to have their cages directly in the sun's rays, because the heat inside soon builds up to a lethal level.

Plastic containers can be very useful, but once again you must make sure to keep them free of condensation by wiping the inside of their lids a couple of times each day. Small plastic containers such as sandwich boxes or empty margarine or honey tubs are, I find, ideal enclosures for incubating eggs or rearing small caterpillars. Don't bother to punch air holes in the lid, because eggs and caterpillars require very little oxygen, and holes could let something nasty creep in.

Good hygiene is extremely important at all times, so enclosures of any sort must always be kept spotlessly clean. It is very helpful to put a flat layer of absorbent paper on the bottom to catch the caterpillar's droppings, called "frass" by butterfly people, and any spilled moisture and bits of waste food. When soiled, it can be carefully lifted out, rolled up, and then burned or put into the garbage can. This should be done no less than once a day. Obviously,

*Short Tailed Swallowtail nectaring from wild iris. Though iris are not generally considered good butterfly attractants, this one is a particularly important nectar source for the Short Tailed Swallowtails of my area.*

if you have a good-sized batch of large caterpillars such as Mourning Cloaks, Swallowtails, or Tortoise Shells, you would in all likelihood remove the paper twice a day. Still, don't keep changing the paper and fiddling about in the cage needlessly, because caterpillars are much better off if left alone as much as possible.

A useful pen can easily be made out of a strong cardboard box standing on its end and with a large window cut out of one or more of its sides. The window should be covered with some very-fine-meshed drapery material, though fly netting will serve if necessary. Years ago black silk chiffon was one of the favourite things to use, but nowadays it is hard to get and very expensive. A few years ago I spent the best part of a day going around the shops in Edinburgh, Scotland, trying to buy some. What I remember most are the odd looks I received from shop clerks when I explained why I wanted it; without fail they thought it a terrible waste to use such material on butterflies! Fly netting will allow good enough light and air penetration, and will keep out the large- and medium-sized parasitic wasps and flies. Unfortunately, it cannot stop the very tiny parasites entering. This is one of the reasons I prefer to keep eggs and small, easily managed caterpillars in airtight plastic containers.

If you happen to be handy or a bit of a carpenter, you may find it fun to build some wooden cage frames and cover them with an appropriate material. If well built and given the proper care, they will last for years, but you should remember that all permanent cages must be sterilized regularly, especially if you have had any health problems among your stock. One of the great advantages of a cardboard box or other cheap, temporary container is that it can be burned or discarded at the end of each breeding season or as soon as you suspect it has been exposed to something harmful.

There are, of course, various manufactured cages available from biological supply houses or commercial butterfly farms. They are designed specially for rearing butterflies, but they may be quite costly, unless they can be used for several consecutive years.

I like using a large walk-in cage, with benches where pot-grown host plants and nectar-supplying flowers can be moved around at will. I do in fact use an old, converted plant propagation pit house 9 m X 3.7 m (30 ft X 12 ft). The main body of the house is below ground, with the plant benches situated level with the surface. The roof comes to a 2.5-m (8-ft) peak, and is covered with fly netting for about two-thirds of its length. The remaining one-third is covered in opaque plastic sheeting so that I can put the plants under cover if I don't want them to get wet. In the winter the whole cage is covered with plastic sheeting.

This converted enclosure gives me a more elaborate setup than is generally needed. I would not have built it just for this purpose, but since it became vacant when we relocated our plant nursery, I decided to put it to good use. Though by no means perfect, it has shown me the value of a walk-in cage for rearing butterflies, so much so that were I to start this hobby again, in my own garden, I certainly would not be long in having one. A walk-in cage need not be elaborate and can easily be made with a few bits of lumber and some fly netting. The important thing is to make sure all the joints are insect-tight, especially around the door, and to site the structure where it can get plenty of sunshine.

Among other things, a walk-in cage allows you to grow the larger host plants such as shrubs and small trees under cover, and lets you hang pots of flowers at different heights. If you decide to keep the adult butterflies in captivity, such a cage would prove invaluable. But I like to let my emerging butterflies out into the garden as soon as possible – one of the main reasons I handle only native butterflies and have always turned down the offer of exotic ones that could not survive at liberty here. One problem with butterflies in cages is that they have a habit of staying close to the top, even in large cages. Though I have had Swallowtails and Red Admirals fly down to feed from flowers at ground level, most do seem to have a compulsion to flutter their lives away at the highest possible point. If you have penned up females for laying purposes, you must therefore hang flowers and host plant samples high up in the cage, where they will be easily located. A small cage is not such a problem, but the plant material, to be effective, still has to reach up very close to the top.

Butterflies that have been reared in captivity are far more adaptable to life in a cage than those netted in the wild and imprisoned. Indeed, provided you can get them to feed adequately, it is good practice to keep hand-reared adults in a cage in the garden for three to four days after their emergence. This gives them a sense of home, so that when you eventually leave the door open and let them fly out of their own accord, there is a good chance they will stay around in the area. Some individuals may even reenter the cage for shelter from time to time. Naturally, if hand-reared butterflies are to stay around, you must provide them with an abundance of suitable flowers growing close by.

Before going out to collect eggs or caterpillars, make sure you have sufficient quantities of the correct food plant on hand. Caterpillars can be reared on freshly-cut foliage or on live plants. I like to use live pot-grown plants, if possible, because that ensures the caterpillars will have fresh food at all times. If you don't put too many caterpillars together on one plant, there is usually enough new growth to keep ahead of the demand. These plants, if perennial, can be maintained in a good-sized pot for several years. A good feeding with a soluble fertilizer early in the spring before the caterpillars are obtained, will keep the plants going all summer, provided they receive regular watering. Make sure you don't get any of the fertilizer on the leaves; if you do, wash it off with clean water. Though caterpillars will rarely eat soiled vegetation, they should never be exposed to artificial chemicals of any sort.

Whether you feed your caterpillars on cut or on growing vegetation, it is extremely important to check it for undesirable livestock before presenting it to them. Aphids, ants, earwigs, slugs, beetles, spiders and so on among the food are all detrimental and should be removed – picked off by hand or blasted off with a fine spray of water. Potted plants should always first be submerged in water to drive out any creatures hiding in the soil. Afterwards, wet vegetation should be allowed to dry before being given to the caterpillars.

A tiny creature can go unnoticed on a spray of leaves no matter how well you think you have checked, particularly with some kinds of flower seed heads that have to be renewed from the wild. Some years ago I was rearing a fairly large larva of a Spring Azure that had recently been brought in to me. It was doing very well in an empty margarine tub, busily feeding away on its main Newfoundland host plant, the flat-topped cluster of wild raisin seeds. One afternoon, seeing that its food was all but gone, I rushed out into the garden, cut a new sprig, carefully checked it for unwanted lodgers and put it in the cage. Since a margarine tub is airtight and since I had put in ample food for one larva, I didn't bother to check it until the following afternoon. Imagine my surprise when I opened the lid and found not one Spring Azure caterpillar, but three! This experience illustrates two points: that I had not checked the newly-gathered food carefully enough, and that the slug-like caterpillars of the Gossamer-winged group of butterflies are extremely well-camouflaged. I was lucky I had not missed a flower spider or the larva of a green lacewing, for that would have meant the end of my caterpillar.

If you feed your caterpillars on cut food in a non-airtight cage, you will have to water the vegetation to keep it fresh and attractive to the creatures. You can do this by standing the plants in a jar of water or wet sand. Some experts advise that wet sand is better because it does not allow the plant to take in too much water and become over-succulent; in my climate, however, wet sand causes the food to wither far more quickly. So far I have experienced no trouble from standing my food plants in water. When feeding your charges in this manner, you must block up the top of the water container around the plant stalks, because caterpillars cannot swim, and they drown very easily. Cotton wool makes a useful plug, though I often fasten a piece of fly screen over the container's mouth, cut in some small slits, and then poke the stems down through them. I have also found that placing a thick layer of clean gravel in the bottom of the container does wonders for its stability. Keeping the plant supplied with fresh water and the container clean both inside and out is important.

Food, whether potted or standing in water, should be positioned so that at least part of it is touching the side of the cage. Since caterpillars that fall off their food are inclined to crawl up and around the wall of the container, this little trick ensures that they find their browse again before becoming too hungry and in danger of a setback. It is very important not to allow anything to prevent the caterpillars from continually eating their fill.

Collecting eggs or caterpillars from the wild requires some knowledge of the desired butterfly's habitats as well as of the kind of plant it lays on. You must develop an eye, because until you train yourself to spot what you are seeking, you will inevitably pass it by. Once you have mastered this skill, however, you will find a surprising number of eggs and caterpillars. When you are searching for caterpillars, look out for signs of their frass or for leaves that have been browsed; these often indicate that a caterpillar is still close by. There are a few caterpillars, those of the Large Skipper of Britain and the Pink Edged Sulphur of North America, for instance, that flick their droppings well away from the area where they are feeding, so looking for the frass of these creatures would be pointless.

Some caterpillars in both Britain and North America produce and excrete a honeydew that is particularly attractive to ants. Therefore, when you are hunting for these, it might be worthwhile to give special attention to any piece of the host plant where ants seem to be showing unusual interest. The larvae of many of the Blues and the Hairstreaks, as well as of the pretty Orange Tip, attract ants in this way.

Because it is very difficult to pick up a caterpillar, especially a small one, with sufficient sensitivity, you should never touch one except when absolutely necessary. Do not carry one around in your hands. It is much better to pick off the leaf, flower, or piece of stem carefully, and transport it with the caterpillar still attached. It can be carried in a small, sealed plastic container or in a brown paper bag, and should be kept away from the sun. Do not carry caterpillars in plastic bags; these bags, if kept shaded, are wonderful for carrying home freshly-gathered foliage, but not at all good for caterpillars. If you have to move a caterpillar, do so on a small-headed, soft-haired, artist's paint brush. Or if the creature has fallen off its resting place, use a spoon to scoop it up and, if necessary, the small brush to push it onto the spoon. You must do all such moving with patience and care. When you are changing the food of caterpillars in captivity, don't try to transfer the caterpillars manually; simply put the fresh browse into the cage so that it is touching the old food. The caterpillars, preferring fresh new growth, will soon move to the better food supply themselves and so allow you to remove the older material. However, if any caterpillar stays clinging in an immobile state to the old food, leave it alone. It is quite possibly undergoing a skin change and should not be disturbed. Simply cut off the leaf or piece of stalk it is on and carefully place this in among the fresh food. When it has undergone its change, it will soon transfer to the new food and start eating. Caterpillars are essentially eating machines, and although they do take time off to rest, they should never be without food to chomp on. Remember, of course, to offer only an amount they can reasonably consume before the food wilts and has to be changed. An overabundance of vegetation in the cage is unnecessary and possibly harmful; it serves no useful purpose and increases your chance of introducing something undesirable. If something unwanted is in the cage, too much browse can prevent you from spotting it in time. Superfluous vegetation can cause increased condensation; it also offers your charges better concealment, and you less chance to have the pleasure of watching them.

When I'm in the garden or countryside, I like to keep an eye open for laying butterflies. By doing so, I not only get eggs to rear, but also obtain firsthand information on the type of host plant, the mode of laying and, in due course, the length of time it takes for a caterpillar to appear. When I find a butterfly laying, I usually collect the leaf with the egg attached and place it

*The Orange Tip is seen here with one of its principal host plants, the cuckoo flower or lady's smock. It is a beautiful British butterfly of roadsides, lanes and woodland edges, that will happily enter the larger, more natural type of butterfly garden.*

in an airtight margarine tub. I leave the stem of the leaf on so that the leaf itself does not lie too flat on the bottom of the container. Before fitting on the lid I give a quick puff of breath into the container, and I do this whenever I open the tub to inspect its contents. This quick breath provides just enough humidity to keep the leaf fresh and the egg from drying out. I also use this technique with tiny caterpillars in small airtight containers. But be careful not to overdo it with heavy breathing, or you could cause condensation. And although I'm not sure, I think it would be wise to avoid blowing in alien fumes caused by alcohol, tobacco, or garlic!

When caterpillars are large enough for me to see fairly easily, I transfer them onto a live plant. A live plant is more natural, and a guarantee that their food is fresh. To do so, I simply cut off the piece of leaf on which the tiny larva is sitting, and attach this piece to the living plant by laying it flat on a leaf and then pushing an ordinary straight pin through the two. The caterpillar has then only to crawl off the piece of old foliage to find a fresh new world. Remember to place these tiny caterpillars on the same part of the leaf you would expect to find them on in nature. For instance, White Admiral caterpillars you should place at the apex of the leaf. In the wild these creatures almost invariably start feeding around and on both sides of the leaf tip. As feeding advances, the central rib of the leaf becomes exposed and isolated, and it is here, lying along this rib, that the caterpillar spends its time between meals. The young caterpillar does this, but the habit grows less pronounced as the caterpillar gets older. Indeed, after its reappearance from hibernation the caterpillar grows more rapidly and is more inclined to pass the time between feeds hiding on a twig.

It is important not to try to rear more caterpillars than you can readily feed. Some of the gregarious caterpillars such as those of the Mourning Cloak, the Milbert's Tortoise Shell, the Peacock and the Small Tortoise Shell consume vast quantities of browse in their later stages, and unless you have a large stock of host plants available, they can very soon run you ragged trying to keep them properly fed. You should therefore curb your enthusiasm and collect only ten or twelve individuals from a brood. Bear in mind that some caterpillars will turn cannibal unless they are given plenty of space and an unlimited, constant food supply. Remember too that the more food consumed, the more droppings produced. And more droppings means more work changing the absorbent paper on the cage floor and more disturbance to the caterpillars. The experienced rearer knows that some of the effort wasted in trying to cater to unnecessarily large numbers of gregarious caterpillars, would be better and more pleasurably spent in rearing small batches of a greater variety of species.

When your caterpillars are fully grown and ready to pupate, they will start looking around for a quiet, secluded spot in which to undergo this change. They will want to attach themselves to something solid and permanent enough to last until the butterfly emerges. Many caterpillars that turn into butterflies during their first summer, such as those of the Painted Ladies and the Red Admirals, will pupate attached to their host plants. Others, the Swallowtails for example, which pass the winter as chrysalids, must find more permanent, sheltered substrates on which to affix themselves. In captivity, of course, they must find a suitable place within the confines of their enclosure, and you must make sure they can do so. Caterpillars often attach themselves to the sides of the cage, and some pupate hanging from the lid. This spot is all right if they are to emerge within a few weeks, but if they are of the type that remains in the pupa stage throughout the winter, it can be a nuisance. I find it useful to put a few rough-barked twigs in the cage when the caterpillars are reaching pupation. Dead spruce twigs are ideal because they have a number of side sprigs and a particularly rough bark. Swallowtail caterpillars use them quite readily; I have on numerous occasions had four or five of these chrysalids attached to one small twig. Twigs allow the chrysalids to be transferred elsewhere without physical disturbance while the cage is cleaned or replaced – something that can't be done if the chrysalids are attached to the body of the cage.

Caterpillars usually become actively restless when ready to pupate, and with a little experience you can tell when they have reached this stage. Some caterpillars, particularly the gregarious Mourning Cloaks, Tortoise Shells and Peacocks, can at this time be transferred to a roomy cardboard box and placed in the dark somewhere. It is important to roughen the inside of the lid so that the caterpillars can get a solid grip and thereby hang down securely. If the caterpillars are of the type that fasten themselves upright with a silken girdle, you can, of course, roughen the sides of the box instead of the lid. Those kinds that emerge within a few weeks, should be placed in a warm, dark place, and must be checked regularly so that when the butterflies emerge they can be taken out into the sunlight and released. Those that overwinter as chrysalids must be stored until the spring in a dry, cold, dark place so that they will not emerge prematurely. Then, three weeks before the adults are expected to be on the wing in the wild, they should be brought out of storage into the warmth and placed in good lighting but never direct sunlight. It is essential to store these chrysalids in the way I have described; otherwise, they will appear at a completely inappropriate time and will have little hope of finding food when they are released. I have received many an anxious midwinter call from people wondering how to keep active adult Swallowtails alive for the four or five months until they can be released into the wild with some chance of survival.

I prefer to keep my overwintering pupae in an unheated, shaded outbuilding, because rightly or wrongly I believe that naturally fluctuating temperatures are best for their healthy development. On one occasion I left approximately three dozen Short Tailed Swallowtail chrysalids outside in their small cages, which had only green plastic garbage bags inverted over them. They were in a shaded site and soon became buried in deep snow. At the proper time, around mid-June, I transferred them to the greenhouse. Later, I was very happy to release the same number of adults into the Botanical Garden.

Chrysalids must be kept at the right humidity, which can be difficult to maintain if you are rearing under completely artificial conditions. This is another reason I prefer to keep them in more natural conditions, outside. If a chrysalis happens to become too dry, its outer shell or skin grows tough, and the emerging butterfly either is deformed or dies trying to break out of an unyielding covering. It is a good idea to spray pupae gently but regularly with tepid water from an atomizer to ensure their proper development, if you are careful not to maintain them in a wet condition. Good air circulation through the container helps to prevent dangerous moulds or mildews, but keep a close watch so conditions don't become too dry.

The caterpillars of butterflies, such as the Spring Azure and the Silvery Blue, that pupate on the ground, should have a layer of organic matter placed on the bottom of their cage so that they can conceal themselves in it when the proper time comes. I prefer to use damp shredded peat; it is reasonably sterile, whereas soil or leaf mould is home to all sorts of microscopic and not-so-microscopic life, some of which can be harmful to caterpillars. Once the caterpillars have pupated, they can be transferred to empty, covered plastic margarine or honey tubs, placed in fresh, slightly damp peat moss, and stowed away in the cold for the winter.

Butterflies emerging from the chrysalis require a good foothold in order to get enough leverage to extricate themselves. They also need something to crawl up onto so that their crumpled-up wings have space to unfurl properly. This is why, if at all possible, chrysalids should not be removed from whatever it is they were originally fastened to. Loose chrysalids can be inserted into the furrows of a piece of corrugated cardboard placed in the bottom of the cage. A rough twig should be positioned with its butt end near the chrysalis and its top high up against the side of the cage.

As soon as its wings have dried and hardened, the butterfly should be given a chance to drink. You can encourage it to do so by lightly misting the cage with tepid water from an atomizer. At this time butterflies usually prefer a drink of water to a feed; once they have had one, however, they should be exposed to suitable nectar-bearing flowers. Place the flowers in the sunshine, or they will be valueless; the butterflies will not visit them in the shade.

One of the great advantages of rearing butterflies in captivity is that, on the whole, a larger percentage survives to adulthood than in the wild. If you are careful and have clean, parasite-free stock, you will in all likelihood finish up by releasing most of what you started with. If you are looking for a nature hobby of some kind, butterfly rearing may be just the answer. I have not said anything about breeding butterflies in captivity because I have very little experience in this area. But it can be done very successfully and is a wonderful way of acquiring parasite-free eggs and caterpillars. If you feel like giving it a try, first read up all you can on the subject; you will save yourself a lot of headaches in the long run. I have included a few relevant texts in the bibliography at the end of the book.

# Some Thoughts on the Conservation of Butterflies

*Whatever befalls the earth befalls the sons of the earth. If men spit upon the ground, they spit upon themselves.*

– Chief Seattle, North American Chimakuan Indian, 1854.

Some people, though perhaps not many of you who are reading this book, may ask, "Why bother to manage, or, for that matter, conserve, butterflies at all?" Why indeed? The answer is not as straightforward as we might think; as with many other forms of wildlife, a butterfly's true value and place in the overall scheme of things is yet to be fully understood. We do know that butterflies, along with some other insects such as bees and hoverflies, are of considerable value as pollinators of flowering plants, some of which are of direct economic importance to us. It has been estimated that sixty-five percent of flowering plants would not be able to reproduce were it not for insect pollinators. We are told also that some butterfly caterpillars, those of the Monarch, the Red Admiral and the Peacock, for example, are in some situations effective in controlling undesirable plants such as the milkweed and the European stinging nettle. We should all be aware that the well-being of the world's plant life is crucial to our own continued existence on earth. Anything, therefore, that affects the land's vegetable cover in any way, whether for better or for worse, unquestionably merits full consideration.

The realization is growing today that the world's insect and plant life is a veritable gold mine in what it offers medical research – information that will help us solve many puzzling problems, substances that might some day be of benefit to us all. A decade ago, for instance, a substance containing an anti-tumour agent was found to occur in the body of a small, yellow Taiwanese butterfly, *Catopsilia crocale*. So here is one indisputable argument for the management and conservation of butterflies. Also, because butterflies are easily observed, they have proven ideal subjects for population studies and have played a part in the formulation of far-reaching concepts in biology – "natural selection," for example, and "the evolution of dominance," that is, the fact that the dominant gene becomes dominant over the recessive gene. Work on these insects has also helped us to understand population genetics, or how genes spread in a population – a subject unquestionably relevant to our study of human genetics.

Butterflies are also valuable because they are extremely sensitive to habitat change. This characteristic, along with their easy visibility, makes them important indicators of the present state of, or any change in the state of, an environment in which they live. We know that if the population of a butterfly species starts to increase or decline in an area, something in the environmental makeup of that area is changing. Like canaries in a coal mine or stoneflies in a trout stream, butterflies may prove to be a valuable early warning system. One example of butterfly reaction to environment change is the disappearance of the Apache Silverspot from many sites in the Owen's Valley of California. The caterpillars of this little butterfly feed on the leaves of the violet, a plant that requires moist ground. When the ground started to dry up, the violets became fewer and poorer, and the Silverspot population dropped accordingly.

Changes to a butterfly's habitat nowadays result more from human activity than from anything else, and are unfortunately more likely to be detrimental than beneficial to the local butterflies. Human beings now seem to be bent on modifying all the habitable natural areas of the earth, with no real concern for other life forms nor sense of the consequences for humankind. For butterflies, whales, humans, every species, there is a minimum size of habitat necessary if the species is to maintain healthy, viable populations. Since the destruction of natural habitats is irreversible, such destruction not only will bring about the extinction of wildlife species, but also will create an ecological time-bomb for human beings. Whether or not we like to admit it, we are not so far removed from primitive nature that we can ignore the fundamental rules governing all life on earth. We cannot live in isolation, independent of the multitude of other living organisms. If it is to continue on earth, the butterfly must have its required habitat maintained in a healthy, viable condition; if we are to continue on earth, we too must have our habitat maintained – and perhaps the first step is to insist on the conservation of the "lesser" creatures like butterflies, and their habitats. Anybody familiar with the countryside and able to think, will understand some of the unexpected, often frightening implications of our improperly-planned activities. Probably the greatest impact on the countryside, whether in North America, Britain, India, China, Brazil, or elsewhere, has come from a need – sometimes real, sometimes assumed – for more land to produce food and for more trees to feed the insatiable appetite of the developed countries for lumber, paper and other wood products. Of course, neither the problem nor its solution is simple; I would hate to be making the economic and political decisions on such matters. But it is a sign of hope that, whereas twenty years ago the environment was given little attention, now, partly because we have at last realized that much environmental change is irreversible, many authorities including the United Nations are having to give it very serious attention indeed.

*The natural and the artificial are in harmony here, and the old ruined wall seems a part of the meadow itself. Both North American and British butterflies enjoy the wildflowers in this nostalgic idealization, which evokes memories of the countryside in a quieter, less hectic age.*

To return to butterflies, one way we have changed their habitat in North America and Britain is by ploughing up large, often vast, areas of ground to plant extensive patches of a single crop. By creating these monocultures, we have destroyed habitat diversity and so have displaced countless numbers of different animals and plants. By breaking the prairie sod and replacing it with miles and miles of wheat or other single crop, the North American farmer has pushed the prairie flowers and butterflies off huge areas of their range. In Britain, where farm sizes are miniscule in comparison, the farmers have nevertheless grubbed out the dividing hedgerows to enlarge their fields, and in so doing have destroyed the homes of many and varied wildlife species dependent on these ribbons of greenery. It has been estimated that the British countryside lost 7 242 kilometers (4 500 miles) of hedgerow between 1973 and 1977 alone! Though originally an artificial habitat, the hedgerow has long since acquired its own associate plants and animals. One such creature is the partridge, a small gamebird with a fondness for putting its nest in a hedge bottom and for feeding on the insects and weed seeds associated with the grasses and wildflowers growing along the hedge.

I spent a number of my early years in Britain as a gamekeeper working with partridges and pheasants, and I think that many of the features of the countryside of value to these birds are also of value to butterflies, certainly in Britain itself. Hedgerows and rough woodland edges with grasses and wildflowers, wide sunny rides criss-crossing the woodlands, and rough, neglected, bramble-clogged corners – these are habitats that benefit both gamebirds and butterflies. The so-called "poor" farming practices were best for partridges and butterflies. Modern "efficient" farming is not conducive to a species-rich natural countryside.

The use of insecticide and herbicide sprays adds further to the decline of butterflies, partridges and countless other life forms. Butterflies suffer both by coming into direct contact with these chemicals and in the loss of their host plants and the nectar-producing flowers they require. Many of the so-called cornfield flowers of Britain such as the corn cockle are now becoming rare. But there may yet be hope. A recent experiment (1983) in Hampshire in which 6-metre (20-foot) strips around the edges of cereal fields were left unsprayed with herbicide, resulted in a threefold increase in young partridges without any measurable reduction in crop yield. For a few critical weeks after hatching, these chicks are dependent on the insects that live on the weeds of cereal crops. Under normal conditions thirty-one percent of the diet of an adult partridge is made up of weed seeds. Stop to make the comparison with butterflies, who also require wildflowers and "weeds" – this is the sort of consideration that leads me to believe that what is good for gamebirds in Britain is also good for many British butterflies, and we could undoubtedly think of a North American parallel. It is good to know that on some British sporting estates the orders have now gone out that the farm headlands, those strips left unploughed at the end of fields, must be left unsprayed. And none too soon, either!

In Newfoundland the forest industry has recently received government approval for spraying herbicide over a tract of forest, in an experiment to increase the growth of conifers by killing off the competing deciduous growth such as birch, aspen and poplar. If this practice becomes widespread, it will directly endanger our moose and snowshoe hare, and indirectly harm our salmon, trout, lynx, bear and much else. It will destroy the browse for the caterpillars of our White Admirals, Compton Tortoise Shells, Tiger Swallowtails and so on. All this in the name of more pulp and paper – which will end up in useless flyers sent out by businesses pushing unwanted wares, and so be consigned to the waste basket. Lord, what fools we mortals be!

In fairness, it is not just the farming and forest industries that are to blame for the destruction of butterfly habitats. Land developers also take their toll. The need for more homes, airports and roadways is often very real, so land is developed and its associated wildlife destroyed. Much of this development may be unavoidable, but much is needless, badly researched, or haphazardly undertaken.

Prime residential sites are often valuable natural areas containing most if not all of the available habitat of an endangered species. American butterfly conservationists in California are currently fighting hard to save important habitats of the Mission Blue, the El Segundo Blue, the San Bruno Elfin and the San Francisco Silverspot butterflies. In 1984 the British Butterfly Conservation Society tried to persuade the country's department of transport to reconsider their plans to extend the M4 Motorway through the centre of a site that harboured 37 of the 64 species of British butterfly. Habitat destruction in the name of progress is an insidious, worldwide disease. We have, fortunately, some dedicated people trying to police this activity. But their efforts, through no fault of their own, are sometimes a cry against the wind. Active conservationists are few and usually poor, whereas the opposition more often than not is both politically and economically extremely powerful. Those of us who really care about our green and living world should offer the reputable conservation organizations whatever help we can.

One notorious example of a butterfly habitat destroyed by development is the case of the Xerces Blue, which I mentioned earlier. Restricted to sand dune areas on the San Francisco Peninsula from near Twin Peaks to North Beach and from the Presidio southwards to Lake Merced, the colonies of this small, highly specialized butterfly were situated too near San Francisco developers to be left in peace. When in 1943 an expanding military facility claimed the land where the last colony lived, the Xerces Blue became extinct. The area where this little butterfly lived is exposed to cold summer fogs that drift in constantly from the Pacific. For the butterfly to have extended its range and possibly survive, it would have had to adapt to markedly warmer and sunnier weather, and this it was apparently unable to do. This sad story illustrates two important points: first, that a species restricted to a very small specialized habitat can easily be wiped out by human activity, and second, that not all butterflies can withstand as much heat and sunshine as we commonly suppose.

Some people like to blame collectors for any decline in butterfly populations. The facts, however, do not support their contention, except possibly where rare or small, isolated populations are involved. It goes without saying, though, that a collector should do nothing to endanger the continued well-being of any butterfly species. There is one butterfly group that until fairly recently was in imminent danger from collectors – the Birdwing butterflies (*Ornithoptera, Trogoderma* species) of Papua New Guinea. They are still in great demand by collectors of natural history specimens, but fortunately the government there has brought in a strong legislative and management program to save them. Indeed, Papua New Guinea, which gained its independence as late as 1975, is one of the very few countries, possibly the only country, in the world to specify insect conservation as a national objective in its constitution. I myself have no interest in butterfly collecting, and though I sometimes have to collect an odd specimen or two, I much prefer the skill and excitement of trying to "capture" these beautiful, often elusive creatures on film.

Though collecting is on the whole fairly harmless to butterfly populations, there are other recreational pursuits that are not. Ordinary people "having a good time" have brought about the destruction of many a natural site of value to birds, wildflowers, or butterflies. Sometimes the ground is torn up by trail bikes and other all-terrain vehicles, and often sensitive habitats are trampled to death by careless, unthinking hikers and picnickers. Many wildfires on both sides of the Atlantic that destroy vast tracts of countryside result from negligence on the part of people who shouldn't even be allowed near a box of matches! I may sound harsh, but after more than thirty years of having to do with people in natural or near-natural areas in Britain and North America, I am still witnessing new examples of ignorance and carelessness towards wildlife and the countryside in general. Fortunately for us all, there are many who appreciate the wild places and who are keen to do whatever it takes to ensure the continued presence of the natural things they love. By and large, remoteness from nature rather than malicious destructiveness is at the root of abuse of the countryside.

There is no doubt – and I hope I have succeeded in making this point – that the continued existence of any plant or animal depends more on the survival of its natural environment and of its ecological integrity than on anything else. Butterflies are no exception.

*Butterflies of the family* Heliconiidae *gather around a twinning vine of their host plant, the passionflower. Though there is one species that breeds in the southern United States, Heliconids are essentially neotropical butterflies. Enormous variety may exist within a single species, so this is a very difficult group to identify. Heliconids tend to congregate in large numbers in sunny jungle clearings, and are known to form "sleeping assemblies" at night. The passionflower has evolved two mechanisms to protect itself from being over-browsed by the caterpillars of this butterfly. It produces tiny spindle-shaped nodules on its stems similar to Heliconid eggs; gravid females searching for ovipositing sites see these "eggs" and pass on to find sites that are more available. Also, these nodules excrete a sweet fluid that attracts ants, and the ants discourage butterflies from settling nearby. Clockwise from the bottom are* Heliconius sapho *Dry,* H. melpomene s. *sp.* cythera *Hew,* H. erato *L,* H. charitonius *L, and* H. melpomene *L.*

Throughout the world many butterflies are in serious need of help if they are not to become just another memory. But suppose we could get all the governments, industrialists, farmers, land developers and recreationalists to agree on this point; would it guarantee that the world would not lose its butterflies? I think not. It would without doubt be a tremendous step in the right direction, and might perhaps slow down much of the current rate of habitat loss. What if we could put vast tracts of natural butterfly habitat, protected from all interference, aside for them? This might be the answer in regions like the Amazon jungle, but not in the densely-populated, highly-manipulated countryside found in much of Great Britain. Naturally, suitable land must be set aside wherever we want to maintain these insects, but simply reserving land is not enough; we must also manage it properly. In vast wild spaces like those found in Brazil, Mexico, or Papua New Guinea, where a purely naturally-evolved ecosystem still exists, it may be that stopping logging and other development would sufficiently protect the indigenous butterflies. But natural changes in the environment would still take place, and species eventually be lost on that account. We would have to accept their loss, like it or not.

In Britain, where so much of the wonderful diversity of habitats has resulted from past human activities – activities that have been changed drastically in recent years – the ecosystem is neither so ancient nor so stable. If they are to survive there, butterflies require much more of a helping hand. Yet we must realize that whatever we do to conserve butterflies must be compatible with legitimate human needs. We must find a way to reconcile the requirements of butterflies with our own. We can start by becoming familiar with suitable management techniques and with the environmental requirements of the butterflies we wish to assist. There's the rub; at the moment we know very little about these subjects, and it will take a sustained, worldwide research effort by many scientists before we can even begin to fill in the gaps.

As everybody knows, research takes a long time and often huge amounts of money, both of which, as far as butterfly conservation is concerned, are at a premium. Fortunately, there is some funding being made available. Governments in Britain and the United States finance some butterfly research. Privately-sponsored organizations such as the World Wildlife Fund, the Xerces Society of the United States and the British Butterfly Conservation Society also finance what research they can afford. None of this is nearly enough, but it is a start, a good one, a hope for the future.

Sometimes research has unravelled a problem too late for us to do anything about it. This happened with the Large Blue, a British butterfly I mentioned earlier. It became extinct in 1979, only 184 years after its discovery. After many years of painstaking, dedicated research, the information to save it was on hand but was unfortunately not in time to beat the clock. The Large Blue's life history was complex and quite unusual. Its eggs were stuck to the flowers of wild thyme, an aromatic creeping plant of short-turf grasslands. When it hatched, the tiny caterpillar would bore into a flower and feed for three weeks or so. One evening, when it was still quite small, the caterpillar would drop to the ground and secrete honeydew to attract ants. Ants, as we know, are very partial to this liquid, so would quickly gather round, milking it for all it was worth. This didn't harm the caterpillar but did get it well and truly covered in ant scent. In this condition the caterpillar would pull off a rather clever confidence trick. In mimicry of the ants' own larvae it would blow itself up so that it looked, smelled and even felt like an ant grub. Faced with what they thought was one of their own youngsters out and about and unprotected, the ants would go into a tizzy and quickly drag it down into the nest out of harm's way. The caterpillar would then live off the fat of the land simply by chomping away on ant grubs! After a while it would hibernate where it was, and later, in the spring, it would reawaken to start feeding on more ant grubs. Eventually it would form a chrysalis, and shortly thereafter would emerge underground as an adult butterfly. Emergence took place very early in the morning, when the adult ants were fairly inactive, so that the butterfly could crawl up to the surface and beat a hasty retreat before the ants realized what was happening.

Now all this may sound fairly straightforward – though a fine piece of detective work on the scientists' part – but it was not. It seems that only one species of red ant, *Myrmica sabuleti*, was involved, and that this ant is confined almost entirely to sites with the very shortest turf. Apparently just an extra 1.3 centimetres (0.5 inch) in the height of the grass can cause this particular species of ant to die out in an area. Too long a grass also smothers out what was the Large Blue's host plant, wild thyme. Close-crop grazing is essential to the welfare of the ants and of thyme, and so it was to the Large Blue butterfly. Heavy grazing by cattle, ponies, sheep, or rabbits would have kept the grass short enough, but for one reason or another farm grazing was reduced, and rabbits were all but eliminated by myxomatosis. The grass grew long, and the habitat became unsuitable for this butterfly. Scientists discovered the interrelationship among the butterfly, the ant, the thyme and the short turf just too late to bring about the butterfly's comeback. Nor did it help that half of the known sites of the Large Blue had been destroyed over the previous few years by ploughing or other disturbances. Even at the best of times the butterfly's survival rate was low. With the wrong kind of red ant, only 1 butterfly larva out of 30 survived, and with the right species, still only 1 out of 10 made it to adulthood. Not very promising odds.

On a happier note – and keeping fingers crossed – it now seems that British scientists have discovered the means to save the Black Hairstreak from extinction. This small butterfly has been losing ground steadily over the last few decades; it has been estimated that there are now fewer than thirty colonies left in Britain. But scientists now know the reason for the decline, and the habitat characteristics needed to promote the butterfly's comeback. This species is invariably associated with high densities of blackthorn in sheltered, unshaded woodlands. The drastic change in woodland management since World War II, particularly the swing over to conifer plantations, brought about a rapid loss of this type of environment. Now that the requirements are known, steps can be taken to rectify the situation. Fortunately, a number of nature reserves are now building habitats suitable for this butterfly, with admirable results.

It is also gratifying to know that some large industrial corporations are not always the ogres we think. Some years ago there was discovered a manageable population of the endangered El Segundo Blue on land owned by Standard Oil of California, Inc. Representatives of the Xerces Society approached the company's administration in an endeavour to preserve the site, threatened by dune-buggies and sand-removers. Standard Oil not only immediately erected a high chain-link fence around the site, but also removed an alien plant that was crowding out the butterfly's host plant and, furthermore, granted access to researchers. This story shows not only that the Xerces Society is really "on the ball," as we say in North America, but also that much can be accomplished when two groups of intelligent individuals, even ones with totally different priorities, sit down together and discuss a problem sensibly. Such examples may be but small skirmishes in the overall war to conserve butterflies, but I find it very heartening to hear of such things – and Lord knows we nature lovers need as much cheering up as we can get these days!

I sometimes wonder what has happened to us. Why have we, people privileged to live in a "have" society, allowed ourselves to become so divorced from nature? Why have we allowed ourselves to be seduced by materialistic desires, at the expense of a consideration for the well-being of other living things? Do we think we can live in isolation from nature, oblivious of the effect on it of our own actions? Butterflies have been a part of humanity's cultural heritage far longer than many of our modern civilizations have existed. They were, for instance, represented in Egyptian tomb paintings as early as 1400 BC, and they are also woven into the fabric of the spiritual inheritance of the Japanese. A butterfly entering a house in Japan is considered lucky; it is looked upon as an embodiment of the soul of a dead person, bringing luck and protection. At the other extreme, I have been in houses in North America where the homeowner's first response to a butterfly fluttering against a windowpane is to reach for an insecticide aerosol!

A pair of butterflies is a standard symbol at Japanese weddings; the two butterflies, present in symbol, are regarded as officiating at the ceremony and as accompanying the young couple who embark upon life's journey, as fluttering ahead to lead them into a magical flowering garden. If for us, as for the Japanese, butterflies were a symbol of happiness, maybe we would not so blatantly disregard their welfare. For some of us, butterflies do trigger memories of the sunny, carefree days of childhood, but unfortunately the interest too often stops there.

Incidentally, the Japanese are also known for their gift of bringing an atmosphere of peace and tranquillity to a garden. I have never been in Japan,

*Approximately 700 species of Swallowtail butterfly and 300 species of hibiscus are known at present. Because of their large size, active behaviour and beautiful colouration, Swallowtails have probably aroused more human interest and enthusiasm than any other family of* Lepidoptera. *Here, we see two Japanese Swallowtails,* Papilio bianor *Cr and, in the bottom right corner,* Papilio maackii *Ménétr, investigating the gorgeous flowers of hibiscus.*

but I gather the gardeners and horticulturists there are masters at working with the natural environment rather than against it, as we so often do. It would be interesting to know what they do or could do as butterfly gardeners.

I shall probably never get to Papua New Guinea to see the Birdwing butterflies, but I find it reassuring that some steps are now being taken to protect these fantastic creatures from extinction as a result of the depredations of developers and racketeers. One of the methods being used, and the one that takes my fancy, is the encouraging of villagers in many parts of the country to engage in "butterfly farming." Wild female butterflies are attracted to cultivated nectar flowers and provided with host plants to lay on. The resulting eggs, caterpillars and chrysalids are carefully tended until the adult butterflies emerge. The villagers sell part of this crop and release the remainder back into the wild. It is permissible to farm only certain species, and others have complete protection in habitat preserves. The whole undertaking illustrates how, with careful planning and management, a wildlife crop can be taken without undue damage to the population; it is a fine example of how human needs and desires can be made compatible with conservation.

As if the butterfly's existence on earth was not fragile enough they, to say nothing of other wildlife and plants, now have the problems of acid rain and global warming to counter. Mind you, it seems to me that the various scientists disagree as to what is really happening, one way or another. We know that acid raid has destroyed the aquatic life of many lakes but does it, I wonder, make the browse required by caterpillars unpalatable? Can it physically damage fragile eggs and tiny larvae by washing down on them?

I am told that if you put six scientists in a room together and asked them to predict the world's meteorological future you would get six different answers! This, if nothing else, shows just how complex the situation is. Some scientists insist that the world is warming up due to the greenhouse effect brought about by man-made emissions while some still insist that we are heading for another ice age. As a non-scientist I find this all very confusing and really do not know who or what to believe. Irrespective of which school of thought is correct it does not bode well for butterflies. The world's scientists and governments should put their heads together to rectify such problems that, in the final analysis, affect us all.

Vast numbers of butterflies and other wild creatures are in very real danger of being wiped from the face of the earth. The knowledge of their plight is not only depressing but exasperating, especially because most of us feel so powerless to help. We can donate to conservation organizations, but for many of us this just isn't enough to quell our inner anxiety. What then can you and I, ordinary people, do to be of practical help to butterflies? My advice is that you start a butterfly garden, now. And my hope is that this book will help you to make a go of it, and so be of some small benefit – to you, to the butterflies and to us all.

# Appendix

## Scientific Names of the Butterflies Mentioned in the Text

| | |
|---|---|
| **Skippers** | *Family Hesperiidae* |
| Arctic (Checkered) Skipper | *Carterocephalus palaemon* Pallas |
| Large Skipper | *Ochlodes venata* Bremer & Grey |
| Peck's Skipper | *Polites coras* Cram |
| European (Essex) Skipper | *Thymelicus lineola* Ochsenheimer |
| **Swallowtails** | *Family Papilionidae* |
| Short Tailed Swallowtail | *Papilio brevicauda* Saunders |
| Giant Swallowtail | *P. cresphontes* Cramer |
| African Mocker Swallowtail | *P. dardanus* Broun |
| Canadian Tiger Swallowtail | *P. glaucus canadensis* Rothschild & Jordan |
| English Swallowtail | *P. machaon* Linnaeus |
| Black Swallowtail | *P. polyxenes asterius* Stoll |
| Anise Swallowtail | *P. zelicaon* |
| **Whites and Sulphurs** | *Family Pieridae* |
| Orange Tip | *Anthocharis cardamines* Linnaeus |
| Great Southern White | *Ascia monuste* Linnaeus |
| Clouded Yellow | *Colias croceus* Geoffroy |
| Alfalfa | *C. eurytheme* Boisduval |
| Giant Sulphur | *C. gigantea* Strecker |
| Pink Edged Sulphur | *C. interior* Scudder |
| Pelidne Sulphur | *C. pelidne* Boisduval & Leconte |
| Little Sulphur | *Eurema lisa* Boisduval & Leconte |
| Brimstone | *Gonepteryx rhamni* Linnaeus |
| Wood White | *Leptidea sinapis* Linnaeus |
| Cloudless Sulphur | *Phoebis sennae* Linnaeus |
| Small (Cabbage) White | *Pieris rapae* Linnaeus |
| **Gossamer-winged Butterflies** | *Family Lycaenidae* |
| Brown Argus | *Aricia agestis* Denis & Schiffermuller |
| Brown Elfin | *Callophrys augustinus* Westwood |
| Holly Blue | *Celastrina argiolus* Linnaeus |
| Spring Azure | *C. a. pseudargiolus* Boisduval & Leconte |
| Small Blue | *Cupido minimus* Fuessly |
| El Segundo Blue | *Euphilotes battoides allyni* Shields |
| Eastern Tailed Blue | *Everes comyntas* Godart |
| Harvester | *Feniseca tarquinius* Fabricius |
| Silvery Blue | *Glaucopsyche lygdamus couperi* Grote |
| Xerces Blue | *G. xerces* Boisduval |
| Mission Blue | *Icaricia icarioides missionensis* Hovanitz |
| San Bruno Elfin | *Incisalia fotis bayensis* Brown |
| Northern Blue | *Lycaeides argyrognomon* Bergstraesser |
| Large Copper | *Lycaena dispar batavus* Oberthur |
| Dorcas Copper | *L. dorcas* Kirby |
| Bog Copper | *L. epixanthe phaedra* Hall |
| Small Copper | *L. phlaeas* Linnaeus |
| Adonis Blue | *Lysandra bellargus* Rottemburg |
| Chalkhill Blue | *L. coridon* Poda |

| | |
|---|---|
| Large Blue | *Maculinea arion* Linnaeus |
| Arctic Blue | *Plebejus aquilo* Boisduval |
| Silver Studded Blue | *P. argus* Linnaeus |
| Saepiolus Blue | *P. saepiolus* Boisduval |
| Common Blue | *Polyommatus icarus* Rottemburg |
| Purple Hairstreak | *Quercusia quercus* Linnaeus |
| Acadian Hairstreak | *Strymon acadica* Edwards |
| Striped Hairstreak | *S. liparops* Boisduval & Leconte |
| Black Hairstreak | *Strymonidia pruni* Linnaeus |
| White Letter Hairstreak | *S. w-album* Knoch |
| Arota Copper | *Tharsalea arota* Boisduval |
| | |
| **Heliconids** | *Family Heliconiidae* |
| Zebra | *Heliconius charitonius* Linnaeus |
| | |
| **Brushfooted or Nymphalid Butterflies** | *Family Nymphalidae* |
| Small Tortoise Shell | *Aglais urticae* Linnaeus |
| Purple Emperor | *Apatura iris* Linnaeus |
| Silver Washed Fritillary | *Argynnis paphia* Linnaeus |
| Hackberry | *Asterocampa celtis* Boisduval & Leconte |
| Silver Bordered Fritillary | *Boloria selene terraenovae* Holland |
| Purple Wing | *Eunica* sp. |
| Marsh Fritillary | *Eurodryas aurinia* Rottemburg |
| Peacock | *Inachis io* Linnaeus |
| "British" White Admiral | *Ladoga camilla* Linnaeus |
| Viceroy (Mimic) | *Limenitis archippus* Cramer |
| "North American" White Admiral (Banded Purple) | *L. arthemis* Drury |
| Red Spotted Purple | *L. a. astyanax* Fabricius |
| Lorquin's Admiral | *L. lorquini* Boisduval |
| Heath Fritillary | *Mellicta athalia* Rottemburg |
| Mourning Cloak (Camberwell Beauty) | *Nymphalis antiopa* Linnaeus |
| Milbert's Tortoise Shell | *N. milberti viola* dos Passos |
| Large Tortoise Shell | *N. polychloros* Linnaeus |
| Compton Tortoise Shell | *N. vau-album* Denis & Schiffermuller |
| Pearl Crescent | *Phycoides tharos arctica* dos Passos |
| Hop Merchant | *Polygonia comma* Harris |
| Green Comma | *P. faunus* Edwards |
| Hoary Comma | *P. gracilis* Grote & Robinson |
| Question Mark | *P. interrogationis* Fabricius |
| Oreas Angle Wing | *P. oreas* Edwards |
| Grey Comma | *P. progne* Cramer |
| Satyr Angle Wing | *P. satyrus* Edwards |
| Zephyr Angle Wing | *P. zephyrus* Edwards |
| Buckeye | *Precis lavinia* Cramer |
| Atlantis Fritillary | *Speyeria atlantis* Edwards |
| San Francisco Silverspot (Callipe Fritillary) | *S. callippe* Boisduval |
| Apache Silverspot (Nokomis Fritillary) | *S. nokomis apacheana* Skinner |
| Red Admiral | *Vanessa atalanta* Linnaeus |

| | |
|---|---|
| Painted Lady | *V. cardui* Linnaeus |
| American Painted Lady | *V. virginiensis* Drury |
| **Satyrs and Wood Nymphs** | *Family Satyridae* |
| Ringlet | *Aphantopus hyperanthus* Linnaeus |
| Wood Nymph | *Cercyonis pegala* Fabricius |
| Inornate Ringlet | *Coenonympha inornata* Edwards |
| McIsaac's Ringlet | *C. i. mcisaaci* dos Passos |
| Small Heath | *C. pamphilus* Linnaeus |
| Disa Alpine | *Erebia disa* Thunberg |
| Mountain Ringlet | *E. epiphron* Knoch |
| Grayling | *Hipparchia semele* Linnaeus |
| Meadow Brown | *Maniola jurtina* Linnaeus |
| Marbled White | *Melanargia galathea* Linnaeus |
| Jutta Arctic | *Oeneis jutta terraenovae* dos Passos |
| Polixenes Arctic | *O. polixenes* Fabricius |
| White Veined Arctic | *O. taygete* Greyer |
| Speckled Wood | *Pararge aegeria* Linnaeus |
| **Milkweed (Monarchs)** | *Family Danaidae* |
| Queen | *Danaus gilippus* Cramer |
| Monarch | *D. plexippus* Linnaeus |
| **Hawkmoths** | *Family Sphingidae* |
| Clear Winged Hawkmoth | *Hemaris thysbe* Fabricius |

## Scientific Equivalents of the Common Plant Names Used in the Text

Also check the list of plant names at the end of the chapter "Flowers for Butterflies."

| | |
|---|---|
| Alder | *Alnus* spp. |
| Alder Buckthorn | *Frangula alnus* |
| Alkanet | *Anchusa capensis* |
| Alpine Azalea | *Loiseleuria procumbens* |
| Antirrhinum (Snapdragon) | *Antirrhinum majus* |
| Apple | *Malus* spp. |
| Ash | *Fraxinus* spp. |
| Aspen | *Populus tremuloides* |
| Asters | *Aster* spp. |
| Balsam Fir | *Abies balsamea* |
| Balsam Poplar | *Populus balsamifera* |
| Beach (Sea) Pea | *Lathyrus japonicus* |
| Beeches | *Fagus* spp. |
| Birch | *Betula* spp. |
| Black Cohosh | *Cimicifuga racemosa* |
| Black Crowberry | *Empetrum nigrum* |
| Black Spruce | *Picea mariana* |
| Blackthorn | *Prunus spinosa* |
| Bluebells | *Hyacinthoides non-scripta* |
| Blueberry (Low Sweet) | *Vaccinium angustifolium* |
| Bog Candle | *Lysimachia terrestris* |
| Bog Candle Orchid | *Habenaria dilatata* |

| | |
|---|---|
| Bog Laurel | *Kalmia polifolia* |
| Bog Rosemary | *Andromeda glaucophylla* |
| Borage | *Borago officinalis* |
| Bracken | *Pteridium aquilinum* |
| Brambles | *Rubus fruticosus,* etc. |
| Bristly Sarsaparilla | *Aralia hispida* |
| Buckthorn | *Rhamnus catharticus* |
| Buttercup | *Ranunculus* spp. |
| Butterfly Bush | *Buddleia davidii* |
| Calypso Orchid | *Calypso bulbosa* |
| Canada (Creeping) Thistle | *Cirsium arvense* |
| Carrot | *Daucus carota sativus* |
| Ceanothus | *Ceanothus* spp. |
| Celery | *Apium graveolens* |
| Chinese Elm | *Ulmus parvifolia* |
| Choke Cherry | *Prunus virginiana* |
| Chuckley-pear | *Amelanchier* spp. |
| Common Privet | *Ligustrum vulgare* |
| Corn Cockle | *Agrostemma githago* |
| Cosmos | *Cosmos bipinnatus* |
| Cranberry (Wild) | *Vaccinium oxycoccus*<br>*V. macrocarpon* |
| Cucumber | *Cucumis sativus* |
| Dandelion | *Taraxacum officinale* |
| Diapensia | *Diapensia lapponica* |
| Dill | *Anethum graveolens* |
| Dogberry (Mountain Ash) | *Sorbus americana* |
| Dog Violet | *Viola canina* |
| Douglas Fir | *Pseudotsuga menziesii* |
| Dusty Miller | *Artemisia stelleriana* |
| Elm | *Ulmus procera* |
| Fennel | *Foeniculum vulgare* |
| Fire (Pin) Cherry | *Prunus pensylvanica* |
| Fireweed | *Epilobium angustifolium* |
| Fountain Buddleia | *Buddleia alternifolia* |
| Foxglove | *Digitalis purpurea* |
| Garden Lovage | *Levisticum officinale* |
| Goldenrod | *Solidago* spp. |
| Gorse | *Ulex europaeus* |
| Hawkweed | *Hieracium* spp. |
| Hawthorn | *Crataegus* spp. |
| Heather | *Calluna vulgaris* |
| Honeysuckle | *Lonicera* spp. |
| Ivy | *Hedera helix* |
| Joe-pye Weed | *Eupatorium* spp. |
| Knapweed (Black) | *Centaurea nigra* |
| Labrador Tea | *Ledum groenlandicum* |
| Lady's Smock (Cuckoo Flower) | *Cardamine pratensis* |
| Lance-leaved Goldenrod | *Solidago graminifolia* |
| Larch | *Larix laricina* |
| Leatherleaf | *Chamaedaphne calyculata* |
| Lilac | *Syringa* spp. |
| Lily-of-the-valley | *Convallaria majalis* |

| | |
|---|---|
| Lupine | *Lupinus* spp. |
| Meadowsweet | *Spiraea latifolia* |
| Milkweed | *Asclepias* spp. |
| Monkshood | *Aconitum* spp. |
| Mountain Alder | *Alnus crispa* |
| Mountain Ash | *Sorbus americana* |
| Mountain Avens | *Dryas integrifolia* |
| Mountain Cranberry | *Vaccinium vitis-idaea* |
| Mountain Maple | *Acer spicatum* |
| Musk Mallow | *Malva moschata* |
| Native Hawthorn | *Crataegus* spp. |
| Nettle | *Urtica dioica* |
| New England Aster | *Aster novae-angliae* |
| Oaks | *Quercus* spp. |
| Ox-eye Daisy | *Chrysanthemum leucanthemum* |
| Parsley | *Petroselinum crispum* |
| Parsnip (Garden) | *Pastinaca sativa hortensis* |
| Pearly Everlasting | *Anaphalis margaritacea* |
| Pitcher Plant | *Sarracenia purpurea* |
| Primrose (English) | *Primula vulgaris* |
| Pussy Willow | *Salix caprea, S. cinerea, S. aurita* |
| Raspberry (Wild) | *Rubus idaeus* |
| Red Clover | *Trifolium pratense* |
| Red-osier Dogwood | *Cornus stolonifera* |
| Rhodora | *Rhododendron canadense* |
| Rockcress | *Arabis alpina* |
| Scotch Lovage | *Ligusticum scoticum* |
| Sheep Laurel | *Kalmia angustifolia* |
| Sheepsbit | *Jasione perennis* |
| Showy Sedum | *Sedum spectabile* |
| Siberian Elm | *Ulmus pumila* |
| Sidalcea | *Sidalcea malvaeflora* |
| Smooth-leaved Elm | *Ulmus carpinifolia* |
| Spanish Chestnut | *Castanea sativa* |
| Sphagnum Moss | *Sphagnum* spp. |
| Stinging Nettle | *Urtica dioica* |
| Sundew | *Drosera* spp. |
| Sweet Gale | *Myrica gale* |
| Tansy Ragwort | *Senecio jacobaea* |
| Toadflax | *Linaria* spp. |
| Tundra Bilberry | *Vaccinium uliginosum* |
| Violets | *Viola* spp. |
| Viper's Bugloss | *Echium vulgare* |
| Whitebeam | *Sorbus aria* |
| White Clover | *Trifolium repens* |
| White Spruce | *Picea glauca* |
| Wild Currant | *Ribes glandulosum* |
| Wild Gooseberry | *R. hirtellum* |
| Wild Raisin | *Viburnum cassinoides* |
| Wild Thyme | *Thymus drucei* |
| Willow | *Salix* spp. |
| Willow Herb | *Epilobium angustifolium* |
| Wood Anemone | *Anemone nemorosa* |
| Yarrow | *Achillea millefolium* |

## Some Recommended Reading

Here are a few books I have found useful. The list is by no means complete, for there are innumerable books on the market today. Unfortunately, not all books will prove reliable or appropriate to your area. So make sure to consult people who have local knowledge of the subjects, butterflies and gardening. It will save you a lot of frustration and possibly expense.


Baines, Valerie. *Glorious Butterflies and their Flora*. Dedham: The British Butterfly Conservation Society, 1993, 39 pp.

Brooks, Margaret; Knight, Charles. *A Complete Guide to British Butterflies*. London: Jonathan Cape, 1982. 159 pp.

Dennis, John V. *The Wildlife Gardener*. New York: Alfred A. Knopf, 1985. 293 pp.

Diekelmann, John; Schuster, Robert. *Natural Landscaping: Designing with Native Plant Communities*. New York: McGraw-Hill, 1982. 276 pp.

Ford, E. B. *Butterflies*. London: Collins, 1945. 368 pp.

Genders, Roy. *Scented Flora of the World: An Encyclopedia*. London: Granada, 1978. 560 pp.

*The Scented Wild Flowers of Britain*. London: Collins, 1971. 256 pp.

Glassberg, Jeffrey. *Butterflies through Binoculars*. New York: Oxford University Press. 1993.

Goodden, Robert. *British Butterflies: A Field Guide*. Newton Abbot: David & Charles, 1978. 144 pp.

*Butterflies*. London: Hamlyn, 1971. 159 pp.

Gray, Dulcie. *Butterflies on My Mind*. Brighton: Angus & Robertson, 1978. 123 pp.

Hay, Roy; Synge, Patrick M. *The Dictionary of Garden Plants*. London: Ebury Press and Michael Joseph, 1969. 373 pp.

Higgins, Lionel G. *The Butterflies of Britain and Europe*. London: Collins, 1983. 256 pp.

Howarth, T.G. *Colour Identification Guide to British Butterflies*. London: Frederick Warne & Co Ltd., 1973.

Howe, William H. *The Butterflies of North America*. New York: Doubleday, 1975. 633 pp.

Klots, Alexander B. *A Field Guide to the Butterflies of North America, East of the Great Plains*. Boston: Houghton Mifflin, 1951. 349 pp.

McClintock, David; Fitter, R. S. R. *The Pocket Guide to Wild Flowers*. London: Collins, 1958. 340 pp. British.

McHoy, Peter. *Anatomy of a Garden*. London: Marshall Cavendish, 1987. 140 pp.

Measures, David G. *Bright Wings of Summer*. Englewood Cliffs, N.J.: Prentice-Hall, 1976. 160 pp.

Newman, L. Hugh. *Create a Butterfly Garden*. London: John Baker, 1967. 115 pp.

*Living with Butterflies*. London: John Baker, 1967. 228 pp.

Oates, Matthew. *Garden Plants for Butterflies*. Hampshire: Brian Masterson, 1985. 52 pp.

Peterson, Roger Tory; McKenny, Margaret. *A Field Guide to Wildflowers*. Boston: Houghton Mifflin, 1968. 420 pp. American.

Procter, Michael; Yeo, Peter. *The Pollination of Flowers*. Glasgow: Collins, 1973. 418 pp.

Pyle, Robert Michael. *The Audubon Society Field Guide to North American Butterflies*. New York: Alfred A. Knopf, 1981. 916 pp.

Ramsey, Jane. *Plants for Beekeeping in Canada and the Northern U.S.A.* London: International Bee Research Association. 1987. 198 pp.

Rothschild, Miriam; Farrell, Clive. *The Butterfly Gardener*. London: Michael Joseph, Rainbird, 1983. 128 pp.

Smart, Paul. *The Illustrated Encyclopedia of the Butterfly World*. New York: Chartwell Books, 1975. 275 pp.

Steffek, Edwin F. *Wild Flowers and How to Grow Them*. New York: Crown, 1954. 192 pp.

Stevenson, Violet. *The Wild Garden: Making Natural Gardens Using Wild and Native Plants*. New York: Penguin, 1985. 168 pp.

Stone, John L. S.; Midwinter, H. J. *Butterfly Culture*. Dorset: Blandford Press, 1975. 104 pp.

Taylor, Kathryn S.; Hamblin, Stephen F. *Handbook of Wild Flower Cultivation*. London: Collier-Macmillan, 1963, 307 pp.

Tekulsky, Mathew. *The Butterfly Garden*. Boston: Harvard Common Press, 1985. 144 pp.

Thomas, Jeremy; Lewington, Richard. *The Butterflies of Britain and Ireland*. London: Dorling Kindersley, 1991. 224 pp.

Vane-Wright, R. I.; Ackery, P. R., eds. *Biology of Butterflies, Symposia of the Royal Entomological Society* 11, 1984.

Vickery, Dr Margaret. *Gardening for Butterflies*. Dedham: The British Butterfly Conservation Society, 1998. 44 pp.

Whalley, Paul. *Butterfly Watching*. London: Severn House Naturalists Library, 1980. 160 pp.

Whiten, Faith and Geoff. *Making a Cottage Garden*. London: Bell & Hyman, 1985. 160 pp.

Worthing-Stuart, Brian. *Collecting and Breeding Butterflies and Moths*. London: Frederick Warne, 1951. 190 pp.

Xerces Society/Smithsonian Institution. *Butterfly Gardening*. San Francisco: Sierra Club Books, 1990. 192 pp.